Laugh with Your Teenager

LAUGH WITH YOUR TEENAGER

Byron W. Arledge

Tyndale House
Publishers, Inc.
Wheaton, Illinois

To Laura

Second printing, August 1986

Library of Congress Catalog Card Number 85-50492
ISBN 0-8423-2102-0
Copyright 1985 by Byron W. Arledge
Printed in the United States of America

CONTENTS

PREFACE

The main objective of this book is to assist parents in being obedient to God's guidance in rearing their children.

The intent is to draw parents into three fundamental activities: prayer, participation, and praise. First, we need to pray without ceasing that God will help us to be the best parents we can be. Second, we need to communicate our love to our child by joining him in some fun activity. Third, we then can praise the child upon his success, no matter how small, in any activity. What better way for a parent to proclaim his love! The results? We probably will have a better relationship with the child, a better feeling about ourself, and progressively a closer relationship with God. In such interaction, we will find the answer to the question most frequently asked of me by anxious parents, "What can I do with my child?" A more secure and competent child emerges from such interaction.

As parents we strive to develop strength within our child so he will be equipped to cope with painful situations. Our child must have the strength and ability to figure out what to do in new, untried situations. This strength grows primarily out of a vital, loving parent-child relationship, which promotes inner faith and instills inner values. As these values are internalized and clarified through daily experiences, the child finds that God's guidance will help him to choose good alternatives. He becomes the moral, spiritual, whole person that is consistent with God's plan. Certainly such an approach is most beneficial to parents who suffer from the unacceptable behavior of a problem child, who also are suffering from guilt, frustration, and embarrassment.

Since this book is directed primarily toward parents, many of the case stories deal with parent-child relationships. Generally, good parenting produces good children, but unfortunately there are times when youth with bad behavior are raised by basically good parents.

In this book I use the pronoun "he" because most of the youth referred to the court are male. The word "child" is a legal term. To me the word "kid" is better used as a term of endearment.

Humor is a prevailing theme on these pages. The book is a collection of stories built upon the structure of an effective relationship model, which I have developed during eleven years of successful counseling of more than 20,000 youth and families in crisis.

My approach is a different, perhaps radical departure from traditional counseling and psychotherapy. It is adapted from and built upon the positive psychological model of reality therapy as presented in Dr. William A. Glasser's book *Reality Therapy: A New Approach to Psychotherapy* (Harper & Row, 1965). In it youth are not viewed as generally emotionally sick and in need of treatment, but rather as sometimes irresponsible and in need of coping strength and guidance. My emphasis is on the goodness available to youth and on God's potential plan for all youth to lead responsible lives. These case stories illustrate the motto: "Better counseling is done over a hamburger than over a desk."

The first chapter, "Rearing Responsible Children," and the second chapter, "Keep On Keeping On," develop nine steps that have proven to be workable and effective in helping parents guide their youth toward responsible behavior.

Chapter three presents the qualities of caring parents: love, faith, fun, and hope.

Chapter four, "How to Avoid Emotional Traps," outlines structure and case studies of (1) the failure child; (2) the depressed child; (3) the hostile child; (4) the suicidal child; (5) the psychosomatic child; (6) the psychotic child; and (7) the grieving child.

"Problem Behavioral Symptoms," the fifth chapter, presents: (1) the unruly child; (2) the delinquent child; (3) the pregnant child; (4) the chemical-abusing child; and (5) the alcoholic child. This chapter also discusses alternative behavior leading to a positive, realistic alternative life-style.

It has been the constant supportive love of my family, Ann, Laura, Krista, and Trina that made this book possible. I gratefully thank my secretary, Mrs. Mollie Jeffries, for reading and typing what no one else could. The staff of the Summit County Juvenile Court Center, Akron, Ohio, and the women of Church Women United of Akron provided a motivating foundation for my cases. My clients have been good enough to let me practice on them, and understanding enough for me to get better. I thank many advisors, including my mother.

Most of all I am ever blessed by the memory of Fr. Paul Selle, whose life was a testimony of how to love and to laugh with even the "least of these."

1

REARING
RESPONSIBLE
CHILDREN

RIGHT SIDE UP

> [Faith] is like a grain of mustard seed, which, when sown upon the ground, is the smallest of all the seeds on earth; yet when it is sown it grows up and becomes the greatest of all shrubs, and puts forth large branches, so that the birds of the air can make nests in its shade. (Mark 4:31, 32, RSV)

At age four, my daughter, Krista, liked to eat bagels for breakfast, spread with cream cheese, butter, jelly, peanut butter, or whatever else was available. Once as I was walking into the kitchen, my wife, Ann, handed Krista the two halves of her much-covered bagel. As Krista turned to go into the breakfast room, one half fell on the floor.

I do not know why there is evil in the world, why kids get sick, why there seems to be so much suffering, or why covered bagels always land—*splat*—face down.

As a good father, I looked the other way and turned to go back upstairs. Too late; Krista had seen me. Ann stared at me with a look that said, "OK, Father Counselor, do something. And it had better be good."

Krista looked up at me with a half smile, half smirk, half frown—the kind of expression only little ones can muster. She examined the floor and then studied the bagel half that was still in her hand.

"Oops," she said. Then she proclaimed, "Look, Daddy, I held onto one!"

I knew then that my little one was both a great theologian and a great psychologist.

The kingdom of God consists not so much of what we don't have as what we do have. It is not what we can't do; it is what we can. Healing begins when we can find and identify the smallest positive element within us, maybe just a smile. We then need to give it to God to nurture. It grows and becomes the greatest; so much so that we and our family can find security within it.

In my work as a counselor I have found that most people are not really prepared for the tasks of parenting. Security is often felt in parent-child relationships when realistic, workable steps provide the basis for caring and for guidance. The steps which I present here are applicable to any relationship, even though here the normal parent-child relationship is emphasized.

These steps are adapted from the positive psychological orientation of William A. Glasser's "reality therapy."

STEP ONE: MAKE FRIENDS

If we expect to raise responsible, healthy children, we need to become involved with them enough to build a good relationship. It has been said that a child can only be helped if he wants to be helped. This is not entirely true. We must choose to be involved and hope and pray that the child will at least remain open to us.

In my counseling experience, I have found that a child usually denies treatment until he is in considerable pain. During initial sessions the child will inform me that he does not have a problem and cannot understand why his parents or an agency has forced him into counseling. Many say that they do not have a problem "yet."

A child is quick to tell of other children who need help more than he does. Blaming is frequent, particularly of parents.

I feel that 90 percent of counseling involves establishing the relationship. If there is no relationship, there is no real counseling. Better counseling is done over a hamburger than over a desk.

God created man partly for fellowship. The progression of the Old Testament reveals God's desire to give us his love and to receive ours. In Isaiah 43:1, we are reminded, "Fear not, for I have redeemed you; I have called you by name, you are mine" (RSV). God became personally involved with us when he sent his only begotten Son into the world to die for us. Jesus stayed involved with us even unto his death. He gave himself so that we might have life, and life more abundantly. Jesus was able to teach and instruct his disciples because they were his friends. As shown in the Gospels, his purpose became clearer to the disciples as he spent time with them, and as their friendship with him grew.

If we are to follow his example, we must get involved with others, particularly our children. We must show them that we care. It is not always easy, but I believe our involvement is part of the Great Commission, "Go into all the world and preach the gospel to the whole creation" (Mark 16:15, RSV).

Jesus has commissioned us to go also into our own world and present the gospel. When we get involved with others, they receive strength from us and from God. We also receive strength because it is in giving that we receive. We, therefore, become vehicles of his love. How can others learn of God's love unless we give help and become involved with them? How can they know, unless they be told?

It would be difficult to overemphasize this first step. As I examine my own life and personal goals, I realize I must take the risk to become involved in others' lives in order to help them.

I frequently explain to a child that God loves him. Most of the time the youth does not believe me because he cannot feel anyone's love during his crisis. As our relationship develops, I am able to explain God's love further.

Making friends is by far the most important step. After a child begins to feel our caring, he is able gradually to experience God's love. I suggest five ways to establish a relationship and to make friends with our children.

1. PRAY

Every day, it seems, a parent tells me there is nothing he can do with his child. Wrong! We can always pray for the child and for ourselves. We can pray for our child before he is born, pray over him as a tiny baby, pray with him every day. And it is never too late to begin praying for a child.

Never underestimate the value or the power of prayer. Prayer always changes the one who sincerely prays. My grandmother, Laura, used to tell me that in her work she did not always have time to stop and get on her knees to pray. Instead she practiced "walking prayers." Walking prayers work for me when I am entering a detention unit and praying, "God, help me to say the right thing to these kids." Sometimes these are the most meaningful prayers. The Bible says that we are to pray "without ceasing," which means we always should pray for our children. We can't just pat them on the head and hope they make it.

In the Old Testament, Hannah dedicated her child, Samuel, to the Lord. She prayed without ceasing and worshiped the Lord. No matter how bad things are, we can still pray. We can pray with our children whenever possible in the morning and at bedtime. We should pray not only during crises, but daily give thanks, ask forgiveness, and seek guidance.

One mother told me she felt she had done everything wrong in the rearing of her children; but one thing she did right: she prayed for them constantly. She also had her children pray with her—that was very important. Today her children are competent and responsible.

Many of the children I work with say that they would rather die than face their family situation or be sent to an institution. And they mean it! Unfortunately, few of them feel the grace of God. These youth need to learn how to pray. I have known detained youth who prayed that a window would open, that a group counselor would drop his keys, that the referee would forget he had been there only a week ago, or that records would be lost. A better prayer would be: God bless me today so that I get along with others and do not get upset and cause a fight.

A definite family closeness can develop as a result of regular prayer and devotions. Personal sharing among family members should enhance the devotions. Reading Bible story books can also be effective; however, they should never become a substitute for actual Bible reading.

God never ordained worship to be boring. Family devotions should move at whatever level the youngest child can accommodate. The devotions could include worship, praise, confession, petition, intercession, meditation, thanksgiving, laughter, and silence. Music adds to a positive spirit; prayer charts may provide structure.

Whenever possible it is a real blessing for family members to pray together in the morning for God's guidance and protection during the day. Family closeness grows through positive traditions—and family prayer should be one of them.

2. BE KIND

> And be kind to one another, tenderhearted, forgiving one another, as God in Christ forgave you. (Ephesians 4:32, RSV)

Snow Boy. The second step in making friends with our children is to be kind. It takes the presence of God for us to be kind when we feel frustrations all around, and when we feel ready instead to preach a sermon. "Be ye kind to one another," also applies to our kids.

As the mother brought the sixteen-year-old boy into my office, she began telling the many things he did wrong. I asked her to be specific.

Every day the mother would mop the kitchen floor. In her opinion, that made her a good mother: "Cleanliness is next to godliness," she said. During the winter her son came home from school, pushed open the back door, and stomped snow all over the kitchen floor. Then he stood on the other side of the room, folded his arms, and grinned as though to say, "I gottcha!" He knew how to get to his mother. The mother's face got red, and she screamed at the top of her lungs, "I try to be a good mother; you just don't appreciate me. Why do you do this to me? God knows I try."

18

All platitudes. The boy loved it; he got the reaction he wanted.

Later I asked him what he did for fun, and immediately he told me that he made his mother angry (which is great fun for many kids). I asked the mother if she thought her screaming helped. She didn't. I asked if she felt better after she screamed. She didn't; she felt guilty. Some people believe that getting feelings off one's chest makes one feel better. Usually it doesn't.

I asked how long she had been screaming at her son. "Sixteen years," she answered—which told me something. I suggested that she stop. That was hard for her to accept. She thought she was supposed to yell. "Everyone else yells." Her mother, grandmother, and great-grandmother had yelled. The pattern had yet to be broken. Besides, what else could she do?

I asked her what was the flavor of the boy's favorite pie. She didn't know, which gave me another clue as to their relationship. My favorite pie is blueberry. I suggested that she bake the boy a blueberry pie the next day. I told her I wanted her to pound out the dough for about two hours. (Ann would say that might be a little long, but I would much rather the mother pound on dough than pound on her boy.) I also suggested that as she was pounding the dough, she pray that God would help her have a better relationship with her son.

The next afternoon the boy carried in more snow than usual on his feet. He pushed open the door, stomped the snow across the floor, stood, grinned, and waited. His mother was ready. She looked directly at the boy and smiled. That scared the kid; he took a step backward. But she had his attention.

She walked over and said, "Son, I love you," for the first time in years. She kissed him on the cheek—for the first

19

time ever. The boy was flat against the wall. She picked up the pie and smiled. The boy expected it to be shoved in his face. Instead she said, "Son, would you like a piece of pie?" Then they sat down together and ate the whole thing. (Later they both told me that neither liked blueberry pie.) As they ate the pie, tension was reduced and some things happened. The boy asked the mother if she meant it when she said she loved him. Her pie got soggy as she nodded her head. The boy smiled and gave a supreme sixteen-year-old compliment: "Well, you're not so bad yourself." The mother offered to bake more pies. Both thought that was a good idea as long as they were not blueberry! The boy offered to mop the kitchen floor, sometimes.

I contend that perhaps more good resulted from the mother's kindness to her son than had happened in all the previous sixteen years of her yelling. There was a great change in both of their behaviors. The mother was smart enough to initiate the change. The boy was wise enough to follow his mother's example.

In being kind we should also remember to be at least as courteous to our children as we are to our Sunday school class members, the PTA, and neighbors.

3. LISTEN AND TALK

He who has ears to hear, let him hear. (Matthew 11:15, RSV)

We not only need to listen to our children's words, but to "listen" to what they do. Words are only a small portion of their expression. We cannot expect a child of five, ten, or even fifteen to communicate like an adult. We must listen to children's behavior. Does a child do anything around the house? Set fire to it? The way he behaves tells us more than what he says. I believe the parents of a sixteen-year-old child should listen 75 percent of the time and talk only 25 percent of the time. Parents say, "My kid never talks to me." We should still continue to sit beside our child in case he does want to talk. Silence is not only golden, it is also therapeutic.

Life seems so busy, so hectic sometimes that we fail to listen and talk with our children. Again I want to emphasize that it is not what we say, but what we do, that makes the difference. An afternoon having fun sledding is worth a thousand words. We must not be too busy to listen.

Gail, the attention-getter. The wealthy sixteen-year-old girl had been referred to the juvenile court for shoplifting. The father pounded on my desk, telling Gail, "You can't go out after six o'clock, you can't date, and you can never have the car again." And on and on. The girl responded by smiling. I noticed the inappropriate affect and I asked her what was happening.

She said, "That is the first time my father has talked to me in over a year."

She looked at her father and said, "I finally got your attention."

Attention is not to be minimized. We can't oversimplify it, saying, "She did it just to get attention." The father admitted to me that he had been too busy for the girl. I agreed with him.

Then he softly said to her, "You know your dad loves you. Look at the nice home you have. Look at the nice car I bought you. You have warmth and enough food." The mature sixteen-year-old girl said, "You know, Dad, when I get up in the morning, even though the house is warm, I do not feel that you love me. When I eat my cereal, I do not think, 'Wow, Dad loves me.' Even though you gave me a car, I do not feel you love me."

She added, rather profoundly, "Do you remember about a year or so ago when you took off one Saturday afternoon and we went fishing, and we didn't even get a bite? I thought you loved me then." After I heard that, I suggested they go fishing that afternoon.

The treatment plan in this case was not to refer them to some type of therapy; it was to get the girl and father to have a pleasurable experience together. We must listen to what is happening with our children, talk with them about it, and then act.

Reflective listening is a foundation for parent-youth communication. It is based upon the mutual respect of two people communicating with each other. Young people must not fear rejection for expressing their feelings. We do not have to agree, but we have to accept their feelings for what they are. Acceptance is clearly demonstrated by words, tone of voice, affect, touch, eye contact, and posture. Sometimes the best listening requires silence.

A child who is upset sometimes loses perspective. Thus we should not confront immediately, but rather reflect and clarify issues in our own mind as a way of helping the child to lay a foundation for problem solving. Once we grasp what the youth is feeling we can learn to mirror the feeling back. We need to let him know the subject is open to further discussion, reflection, clarification, and concern. We must be nonjudgmental.

Every child needs to feel heard in order to trust enough to keep talking. Often it is helpful to use adverbs to reflect the intensity of our feelings. Encourage them to find the right descriptive adverbs.

Reflective listening gives both children and parents time to think. We must honestly try to understand the meaning behind the words. Parents who use reflective listening are less likely to be manipulated by their children because they are less likely to act impulsively as the youth expects. Reflective listening is a new style of communication for some parents, and it makes them feel uncomfortable, even silly. But it works, and it changes us in the process. Remember, God is a great reflective listener, and he is ever patient with us.

4. MAKE 'EM SMILE

Yours shall be everlasting joy. (Isaiah 61:7, RSV)

Fourth, in order to make friends, we must "make 'em smile." For this we do not have to go to clown school or imitate Bob Hope. We must, however, try to bring a relaxed atmosphere into our homes. When we learn to smile, we get results: we get our children's attention.

Jerry's basketball. The nine-year-old boy walked close to the wall in my juvenile court office. He stood in the corner. He had been referred to the court on a shoplifting charge and had been assigned to the Values Program. The volunteer counselor was present to meet the boy and his mother, who was very large. The boy finally sat down, but he held tightly onto a basketball. He did not seem to be breathing.

I smiled and asked, "What do you have there?" He never answered, never even moved. I asked his name. No answer. Telling him my name was Byron, I also introduced the volunteer.

Then the mother shouted, "Tell him what your name is!" I jumped; she scared me.

Repeating my name, I asked the boy what he did for fun. He leaned over the basketball even more. Then the mother shouted, "Tell him what you do for fun!" I told her I played with my kids. I started tapping the basketball. I must have hit it ten times before he finally looked up at me.

"Do you like to play basketball?" I asked, smiling and hitting the ball again. Finally he trusted me enough to let go; the ball bounced on the floor.

With that motivation, I decided we needed a playing field. I asked his mother to leave. For twenty minutes we hit the ball back and forth until finally he hit the window. He uttered, "Oh, my gosh."

I smiled. "Good, you can talk. What is your name?"

"Jerry," he said with a slight smile. I questioned the volunteer about his basketball skills. It had been a while since he'd played, but he was ready. With the mother's permission, I suggested they go play basketball in the court parking lot. The youth seemed excited.

Several hours later the volunteer called me to say that he could not believe Jerry's response. He had smiled, talked, laughed. Later he even talked while he was eating his hamburger. The youth had found a friend who made him smile.

5. TOUCH

> Then again he laid his hands upon his eyes. . . . (Mark 8:25, RSV)

Her father's daughter. "Have you hugged your child today?" is not just another bumper-sticker slogan.

The twelve-year-old girl had been in her mother's custody since the divorce five years before. The father wanted the child, but he was in the Army and had no way to care for her. During those five years the child had lived in many different locations as the mother had moved from one man to the next. The child had not been taught personal hygiene. She ate whenever and whatever she could. She never lived anywhere long enough to make friends. Her education left much to be desired.

The father and stepmother decided to keep the girl once during a visit. Her adjustment was really rough. The parents gave the girl and each other much support to help her make it through even minimal daily routines such as eating.

The father clearly loved his daughter and was able to show her affection. After counseling he learned to spend time doing a variety of activities with her. One Saturday he played football with her and they had a good time. I asked the daughter if they had played touch or tackle. She laughed, smiled, and said, "Trip."

Unfortunately, the father delayed filing for custody. Out of the blue the mother showed up the following Wednesday night and asked the daughter to go with her to California. The girl told her mother she would rather stay and play "trip football" with her father, reporting happily, "He hugged me. He loves me."

After this, the girl was allowed to stay with her father.

A hug makes friends with your child. The five ways I have prescribed above to make friends with our children normally must be followed in the outlined order. Usually a child is receptive to touch only after steps one through four are initiated. The child should at least smile first or hint at some pleasure in response.

It does not take much touching to let a child know you want to be friends. Touch means a great deal to an unhappy child. A handshake a day is not too much. All kids need a literal and verbal pat on the back.

It is surprising how many youths referred to the court for murder will actually force me to touch them. They stick out their feet for me to "trip"; they pull on the cross around my neck; they come up behind me and grab my shoulders; they touch my arm as we talk. They exhibit the biggest of smiles when poked in the ribs.

Along with touch comes the necessity of eye contact. I think youth are more tuned in to eye contact than are adults. To them it indicates sincerity and honesty as well as a means of building relationships.

After talking, listening, laughing, and touching comes fellowship. This means knowing that someone cares, and also that God is with us at all times. We do not have to rely upon ourselves to make that fellowship real; we rely upon the presence of God, the touch of the Master's hand.

STEP TWO: QUESTION THE PRESENT BEHAVIOR

The second step toward a better life is to question the present behavior. The most frequent procedure can be simply to ask the child, "What are you doing?"

> Forgetting those things which are behind, and reaching forth unto those things which are before, I press toward the mark for the prize of the high calling of God in Christ Jesus. (Philippians 3:13, 14, KJV)

Smoke screen. The thirteen-year-old girl was obviously hostile and upset as her mother shouted at her in the court hall. She was not to smoke. She had been assigned to the Values Program.

The volunteer, who was about fifty-five, was excited about meeting her first case.

I'm not sure whether the mother or the child actually heard the procedures of the Values Program given during the initial meeting. The mother was too busy saying her daughter was not going to smoke while she was with the volunteer. According to the mother, the daughter shouldn't be rewarded with fun activities anyway; she needed to be punished. The mother was not impressed with the Values Program's 92 percent success rate on a monthly basis.

The daughter was frowning the entire time, and would not speak. She was probably thinking of being with her friends and plotting to get even with her mother.

When the volunteer went to the home to pick up the child for their first outing, the mother emphasized that they were a "Christian family." The volunteer was halfway out of the driveway when the child reached into her purse and pulled out a pack of cigarettes. The first words the child spoke to the volunteer were, "Where is the cigarette lighter in this dumb car?"

The volunteer asked, "How would you like to go bowling?" The girl found the lighter and dramatically pushed it in and out several times. The volunteer smiled and talked about rolling gutter balls. The girl blew smoke in her direction, as if she were trying to distract her.

The volunteer suggested that maybe after bowling they could go to McDonald's. The girl just coughed.

Volunteer: "Would you like a Quarter Pounder or a Big Mac?" The girl reached into her purse and brought out another cigarette, adding to the first one. She smoked two at once, blowing more smoke in the volunteer's face.

The volunteer choked and asked, "What are you doing?"

The child began coughing, thought for a moment, put both cigarettes in the ash tray, and said, "I think I would like to have a Big Mac."

They went bowling, and then to McDonald's, where each got not only a Big Mac, but also fries, colas, and hot fudge sundaes with nuts.

The two went out bowling and eating for four weeks before I met them for the first month's review hearing. It seemed to me that I was meeting a different girl. She was giddy. She gently teased the volunteer, mentioning something about the Big Macs. The volunteer said I should tell other volunteers about a potential side-effect of the program. During the month she had gained three pounds!

The child and volunteer continued bowling and eating for a second month. During the sixty-day review hearing, the girl was even more excited and certainly more verbal. They had been bowling each week, and each week had stopped to eat Big Macs, fries, colas, and hot fudge sundaes with nuts. All seemed to be great with the child. The volunteer was a little disturbed, however, because she had gained another eight pounds.

The next morning I answered my phone, only to hear a great deal of shouting. It was the child's mother. The previous evening the girl had "let it slip" that during the two months she had been with the volunteer she had not smoked, except for the first night. The mother was incensed, and wanted to know what kind of preacher I was. I told her I was a good one. I could tell she had a different opinion.

She asked what we had been telling her daughter about smoking. I told her I had never mentioned smoking. She wanted to know what the volunteer had been telling her. "Nothing," I said.

She was enraged, and demanded to know what I was giving her daughter, accusing me of possibly giving her methadone.

She shouted, "What is the volunteer giving her?" I thought for a moment, and then told her the volunteer had been giving her Big Macs, fries, colas, and hot fudge sundaes with nuts.

I then questioned the mother as to how often the daughter smoked at home.

"All the time!"

I asked how often she scolded her daughter about smoking.

"All the time!"

No coincidence, I'm sure.

I advised the mother to stop talking about the smoking and take the girl bowling instead. "This girl is smoking continually and that is all I'm supposed to do about it?" she questioned.

In addition I advised her to give her daughter Big Macs, fries, colas, and hot fudge sundaes with nuts. The mother said I was "nuts," but that she would try it.

They had a great time without smoking. I called the volunteer to thank her for what she had done and to inform her that she did not need to continue; the mother had become the volunteer. The ex-volunteer was glad for the girl and the mother and was somewhat relieved. She didn't really have the time to volunteer anymore. She had also joined Weight Watchers. (Fortunately, she's the only volunteer who has left the court for Weight Watchers!)

The volunteer knew the relationship was more important than the symptoms. The child had to make the decision as to how to behave. She had to decide whether she was going to smoke or not—whether smoking was good for her. The girl found that she had a choice. She traded the smoking for a good relationship.

We must never take anything away from anyone without helping to put something better in its place. The girl took smoking away from herself in favor of a good relationship with the volunteer, and then with her mother.

When we accept Jesus Christ into our lives, we ask forgiveness for the past and we begin a new life with him.

Old things are passed away; all things become new. True repentance is seeking God's blessing for the present and his guidance for the future.

In questioning our child's present behavior, we also ask if he or she is living up to the potential God has given him. Is the child experiencing fulfillment? Is he using his talents for God, others, and himself?

Jesus said that he came into the world so that we might have life and might have it more abundantly. We should encourage the child that each of us can have a better life. We can improve our lives: through God's love we can find love. We have been bought by the precious blood of the Lord Jesus Christ. From right now on, we can feel that love; from this moment, all our sins can be forgiven. If we confess our sins, God is faithful. He will cleanse us from all our past unrighteousness. We can live with him in the here and now.

STEP THREE: HELP THINK

> Even youths shall faint and be weary, and young men shall fall exhausted; but they who wait for the Lord shall renew their strength, they shall mount up with wings like eagles, they shall run and not be weary, they shall walk and not faint. (Isaiah 40:30, 31, RSV)

Thinking—meditation—is the third step in treatment, after (1) making friends, and (2) questioning the present behavior. The purpose of the questioning is to allow a purposeful pause. During the pause we wait for the youth to think. We don't think for him. Allowing this pause requires the skill of "waiting patiently for the Lord."

Personal meditation with God is essential to practicing this step.

Thinking first and pausing may also be called "common sense" or "horse sense." Teaching the art of practical thinking can be done while traveling in a car, with "what if?" questions; or while watching television, by asking our children concerning various situations, "Now what would you do?"

Buttoning up. A volunteer taught her child to think. The very proper volunteer was nervous about meeting her first child. Cindy, age sixteen, had been referred to the court for truancy after her father had signed an affidavit of incorrigibility. During the initial meeting the child told me in a matter-of-fact manner of her pregnancy.

The volunteer and child had a couple of visits together before going shopping in a crowded mall for material to make maternity clothes. The volunteer could not help but notice as the girl walked down her front steps that she was not wearing a bra.

The volunteer talked to Cindy about colors and patterns. As they were walking into the mall, the girl unbuttoned an upper button on her blouse. She also seemed to skip instead of walk. As the volunteer was holding a piece of material toward the girl, she noticed the girl had unbuttoned the middle button as well. The volunteer quickly decided the color was not good.

As they left the store, the well-developed girl unbuttoned all the buttons and was almost hopping along. The volunteer suggested an ice cream break.

The boy behind the counter mistakenly gave the girl two scoops instead of one. As they ate, the volunteer remained silent. The girl asked her what was wrong. The volunteer said she was thinking and suggested the girl do the same.

31

It took the volunteer a long time to eat, long enough to look in the other direction while the girl buttoned back two buttons. As they walked into another fabric store, the third was buttoned. The girl found material she liked while she buttoned the final button.

The volunteer knew it was Cindy's decision to button her blouse and her own decision to button her lips.

STEP FOUR:
THE CHILD MAKES THE JUDGMENT

Next we must ask the child, "Is what you are doing good for you?" This is a difficult step. The judgment must be the child's, not ours. Parents, clergy, school personnel, and court staff may all be right in their assessments, but they are not the ones who need to change; at least, they are not the "identified client."

We cannot push or pull a child farther than he is able or willing to go. If we make a judgment and put the child on the defensive, we have gained nothing—even if we speak with the tongues of men and of angels.

I am beginning to understand why God declared that judgment was his. Youth only change when they want to, when they feel the need to, and/or when the pain is so great that they must change. Often many attempts are made to threaten a child into good behavior. If the child has a differing judgment, we try to threaten him into following ours. Sometimes this works, particularly if the retribution is severe enough, and especially if a child has experienced harsh punishment in the past.

However, a child who only "behaves" because of a threat or harsh punishment has not learned the value of good behavior. Instead, he usually develops hostility toward the threatening person.

Certainly this generation of young people is not easily threatened. Their values are different. They do not exhibit much fear. And if our threat is not carried out, or if it is impossible to carry out, we lose even more ground. Instead, we should encourage the child to make a positive decision, which is in accordance with the love of God for him.

We should let children know that all have sinned and come short of the glory of God and of God's potential for them. Because of the way we act, we separate ourselves from God; this separation is called sin. The wages of sin are spiritual death, a lack of peace, and a loss of inner meaning to our lives. Without God's peace, we have no purpose for our existence, for a day or a lifetime.

We have been born winners; we are all born with abilities. We have the ability to accept God and his abundant life. This is the way to true peace.

In our steps to treatment, first we must establish the relationship. Second, we will ask the child what he is doing. Third, we urge him to think about what he is doing. Then, fourth, we encourage the child to make the judgment by asking him if what he is doing is working for his good. Another such question is, "Is this behavior helping you?" Then we wait. Waiting may take a long time. During the waiting we emphasize the previous steps, particularly the step of making friends.

As our relationship develops, we can express our opinions. If we do not have a relationship, the youth won't care about our opinions. Our own testimonial should be open, honest, personal, and brief. Then we must do all of step one that is possible. In this way our Christian values will be demonstrated.

How we live our own lives is far more significant than our ability to make judgments about our child's behavior.

We must provide an example in our lives to help the child grow toward a better life.

Finally, after much relationship building, the child might feel free to say something about his life which indicates that he realizes all is not well. This is the moment we have been praying for. We agree with him and begin to discuss the present situation. We must not let heavy anger or deep depression take over. Instead we push toward step five: the plan.

STEP FIVE: HELP MAKE A PLAN

Now that the child is moving toward responsible behavior, a plan is needed. At this point the counselor can begin to be more aggressive. He will ask, "What can we do together to make this situation better?" The plan should be designed by the youth, in consultation with the counselor. The youth himself will have learned through his struggles some way he can deal with his situation.

O sing to the Lord a new song. (Psalm 96:1, RSV)

All the way home. The young man named Bryan had been in juvenile court several times. I had not seen him for almost two years, since he had married against everyone's advice. Even though I had also advised against the marriage, I told him I would always be around.

One day Bryan called and demanded, "I want you to do something about my wife. I am going to bring her over there, and either you fix her or I will get a gun and fix her."

During the initial sessions I would ask her a question and he would make some kind of noise in reaction. This was very distracting. I asked them if they wanted to learn to get along. They said they did. We discussed many things which could relieve the tension and threats.

She was a waitress; I asked if she could remember ten restaurants they would pass on the way home. She couldn't.

"How about five?" Maybe she could.

He had worked in a service station, so I asked him if he could list ten stations on the way home. He could not, nor could he remember five.

Considering the complexity of the problem and the threats, it probably seemed insignificant to be talking about restaurants and service stations. But in the years they had been fighting, they had not succeeded in anything, and I knew if they could succeed at this simple task, they would at least have accomplished something.

My plan was for them to have one success.

On the way home she rode in the back seat and he rode in the front because they hated each other. When they were halfway home, he said, "There is a Sohio station over there." And she whispered from the back seat, "I see a McDonalds."

They wanted to try to succeed. He saw a Gulf station and she saw a Burger King. They became allies. With a chuckle in his voice, he pointed out the Sunoco station; and then she giggled as she pointed out Arby's.

Then he said, "Isn't he crazy!"—referring to me—and they laughed. They realized it was the first time they had laughed together in over a year.

After they had played this game for a couple of months, she had pointed out 340 restaurants. Now they have gone beyond talking about restaurants and service stations, and have experienced each other's love. Much else happened, and had to happen; but they found a place to begin, with the "restaurant and service station plan." They sang a new song, together—loud and clear.

The Plan

Whatever plan is used must be consistent with what is worrying the person at the moment. The plan also must be realistic to the situation; it must fit the present need. It must be simple in structure, usually consisting of only a few sentences. The plan must require little time, initially lasting no more than a two-day period.

Later plans can be longer. It is important not to complicate the plan by adding insignificant details, such as length of hair or condition of a bedroom. Contracts are written according to priorities, with one theme per contract.

Perhaps more important, the plan must be accomplished easily enough that the youth has a very good chance of succeeding. The plan must be realistic for the particular youth; he must feel he can do it.

Encourage, encourage, and encourage again. Let him know he is not alone. You and God are with him.

> Therefore, if any one is in Christ, he is a new creation; the old has passed away, behold, the new has come. (2 Corinthians 5:17, RSV)

A plan must be simple enough that a teen can feel successful at it; and we must look for the slightest sign of success to praise.

World's worst housekeeper. Brenda was a nineteen-year-old bride; in her estimation, she was the world's worst housekeeper. It took her a long time to find things. She never answered the phone because she did not want to have to look for it. She said it took her all week to get ready for her counseling appointments.

Brenda seemed to have the necessary desire to change, however. When I asked her if there was anything she could do to get the house clean, she said, "I've got it in me. I can go home right now and clean the whole house." She had probably said that many times before. I asked her if she could spend five minutes a day in each room. Eventually, she succeeded.

She needed a plan in which she would be successful. She regulated her cleaning by a clock. After each task, she would repeat, "I did it. I spent five minutes on this room, and look how much better it looks." Soon Brenda felt better about her house and herself. Behold, the new had come!

Some of my clients are so depressed and have such a low level of energy that the only plan I can agree on with them is that they prepare for their weekly sessions. For such youth, the prayer is not, "God help me to have a wonderful life" but rather, "God help me in the next hour to get my shoes on and tied."

STEP SIX: GET A COMMITMENT

> He leads me beside still waters; he restores my soul.
> (Psalm 23:2, 3, RSV)

In this step, results can usually be seen. Tension is often stilled; souls are restored. The commitment usually takes the form of a written contract, and accurate wording is essential. The contract serves to finalize the plan. The contract should do two things: reduce the tension; and meet the "here and now" priorities.

Usually the contract will have no more than three goals. Whenever possible it should be signed.

A child's signature means something; sometimes his name is all that truly belongs to him. When a child signs a contract he usually feels he must go through with it. I sign the contract too, and I ask the parents to sign. Then I ask

37

the child to put his copy of the contract on his door, the bathroom mirror, the refrigerator door, or anywhere he will see it. It is better that the youth be reminded of the contract because of its visibility than because his parents remind him of it. The desire to rebel against parents can work against successful completion of a contract.

Commitment is not the first step. Commitment follows the other five steps. We cannot push youth into step six. Counseling itself is not the process of commitment. Counseling involves developing a relationship which leads to a series of events centering around a commitment.

Van's contract. Van was having serious difficulties with his parents because of his school situation. This child really wanted to complete his education, but he was rebelling against his parents, who were constantly after him about his attendance and grades. The family needed to find some way out of their disagreement about school other than to be constantly yelling at one another.

COUNTY OF SUMMIT JUVENILE COURT
Division of Court of Common Pleas
650 Dan Street, Akron, Ohio 44310

SOCIAL CONTRACT

CHILD: Van Woosley, age 16
PARENTS: Mr. and Mrs. Charles Woosley
DATE: May 3, 1985

1. Van will attend school. All family decisions will be based upon success in school.

2. The curfew agreed upon for week nights is 10:00 P.M., and for Friday and Saturday, 11:00 P.M. When curfews are successfully kept, special exceptions will be made.

3. The privacy of Van's room is to be respected at all times. Van is to have complete responsibility for keeping his room clean.

4. A $5.00 a week allowance will be given for the completion of agreed upon duties. Extra money may be earned from extra jobs.

_____   _____
VAN WOOSLEY   MR. CHARLES WOOSLEY

_____   _____
MRS. CHARLES WOOSLEY   DR. BYRON W. ARLEDGE

It has been my experience that parents also sometimes violate social contracts. For instance, if the contract states that the parents will not yell at the child for missing school, and he fails to attend on a particular day, it does not follow that they have the right to start yelling at him again.

If the original contract does not work, we write another—an easier contract—reemphasizing the goal of the contract, the role of the child, and the role of the parent.

In a social contract, goals must always be carefully defined. Notice the bonus clause. Whenever possible, contracts should be written in positive language. We try to make them short, realistic, attainable, and success-oriented. I cannot overemphasize the need for some immediate gratification and success; the child needs to experience the feeling of achievement, however meager. The contracts should be reviewed at least weekly, and should be discussed by all concerned, openly and honestly.

Another benefit of social contracts is that they give the child a sense of responsibility and allow him to function, at least in some way, as an adult. This helps to build self-esteem and encourages the child to live up to adult standards in other ways.

> For the Lamb in the midst of the throne will be their shepherd, and he will guide them to springs of living water; and God will wipe away every tear from their eyes. (Revelation 7:17, RSV)

Kerry's fear. Kerry was afraid of being with people. The sixteen-year-old boy had been in his basement for eight months, following several traumatic experiences that had reinforced his fear. Fortunately there was a phone in the basement. His father told him about me, but the boy was not at all willing to take the risk of talking to me on the phone—let alone permitting me to visit.

Every day for two weeks, at noon, I called him and let the phone ring three times. The third week I let the phone ring six times. I sent a message to Kerry that on Monday of the fourth week, I wanted him to acknowledge my concern by picking up the phone after the second ring.

On that day the phone rang once, then twice. He didn't pick it up. Three, four, five, six, seven, eight rings before he picked up the phone receiver.

I said, "Hello, Kerry." No response. He hung up.

This pattern was repeated every day for two more weeks. Each time there was a longer period of silence before he hung up. I informed him I was praying for him and I wanted to meet him sometime, whenever he was ready.

After another two weeks, God helped: the boy sneezed. I said, "God bless you," risking a laugh. The most wonderful sound came over the phone. He giggled. Then silence. Finally he said, "Hi."

I yelled, "Wow, hi!" He giggled louder and said a stronger, "Hi."

I said, "Thank you, Jesus." He said, "Thank you, Byron."

I told him the sun had begun to shine in my window and asked if the sun was shining in his. He had me wait while he opened the curtain. He said he was glad to see the sun.

The phone calls continued. A week later he got dressed. A few days later he began his ascension up the stairs, two additional steps each day. It was a long time before I sat in his driveway and saw him wave out the window. It was yet a longer time before we drank a cola together, face to face. I don't think there was ever a more nervous McDonald's customer. No one would believe how I prayed over the meeting.

Getting Kerry to that point took time, and a series of small, realistic goals. He responded gradually to me and to God. And God wiped away his tears.

Before we can have a positive relationship with our children, we must have a positive relationship with ourselves. Naturally, being a good parent gives us a sense of well-being. As a beginning point for success, parents must understand the expectations they place upon their children. These expectations must be realistic, and the child must both understand and agree to the expectations.

How sad it is when parents frustrate their children every day; then parents and children become alienated and feel like failures. Children will never succeed if unrealistic expectations are placed on them. It is no wonder some children rebel and run away; it is easier than facing the pressure of a parent's unrealistic expectations.

On several occasions, after completing and signing a contract, I have asked the family if they would care to pray together that God would help them carry out the contract effectively and meaningfully.

Salvation itself is a commitment. Ideally, the youth accepts God's love and reconciliation through Jesus Christ, so that we can say, "By his strength you will be able to act more responsibly and realistically."

By God's grace we can all be changed—through faith and not by ourselves. It is a gift of God, not our work, but God working in and through us.

2.
KEEP ON
KEEPING ON

STEP SEVEN: HELP MAKE A NEW PLAN

We hope and pray that the first six steps will work toward a commitment. A well-devised plan should work—most of the time. However, sometimes it doesn't, for a variety of reasons.

> We destroy arguments and every proud obstacle to the knowledge of God, and take every thought captive to obey Christ. (2 Corinthians 10:5, RSV)

Valerie's A. A plan that fails can be revised to work if we keep on keeping on. It is important to admit it when we need a more realistic plan.

The high school freshman set the honor roll as her goal even though she was barely making Cs. She was very upset when she did her best and still made only Bs. Her parents were wise enough to highly praise her for her Bs. They did not depress the student by reminding her of the honor roll plan. She decided that during the next grading period, she would work for one A. She fulfilled the more realistic goal and made one A.

When a plan fails, frustration and disappointment often overtake parents and counselors. Then special strength is needed to go back and intensify step one, "Make Friends." We must keep on keeping on. If we give up, the child most assuredly will, too, and possibly become worse than before. Sometimes we need to go through each step again. Then as we are sitting beside the kid watching TV, we can remind him of his judgment to change and ask what he would like to do next. Will it be the same plan or would he like to make a new one? Usually the new plan involves lower expectations than the first. But we must continue to encourage him in the new plan and support him with enthusiasm.

> There is great gain in godliness with contentment. (1 Timothy 6:6, RSV)

Making excuses only undermines the responsibility of the child and of the parent. Doing so lets the child off the hook. The child also perceives that we are not seriously involved. A boy told me he knew his probation officer did not care about him because he accepted "any dumb old excuse." Accepting excuses breaks the relationship of trust.

The bullies. He looked even younger than his ten years as he slowly walked into my counseling office, head bowed, hands in his pockets. He enjoyed talking about fighting. At the first session we also talked about making model planes, and for the second session he brought in his favorite model. Toward the end of the third session he mentioned how his nose hurt a little. I commented that I noticed a little blood. On his own he said that maybe he should stop fighting.

I praised the response. I asked if he could make it through the next day without fighting. He was sure he could, and seemed proud to sign his name to the quickly devised contract. He also agreed that he would call me at 7:00 P.M. the following evening.

I waited. Finally, at 10:00 P.M. the phone rang. He hardly gave me a chance to say "Hello" as he began telling me about all the "big bullies" who kept saying things about his mother; and, of course, he had to stop it.

When I could get a word in, I simply asked if he still wanted to resist fighting. He did. He agreed to call me after his lunch period the next day to tell me how he made it through half a day.

At 1:00 P.M. sharp, the phone rang. He was so excited. He had been successful. But that afternoon two kids did not share his excitement, so he punched them. Still, he knew from the morning's success that he could make it if he really wanted to.

God does not accept our excuses. We must ask his for-giveness, and then he is faithful and just to forgive us our sins and to cleanse us from all unrighteousness, so that we can begin again with a new plan, a new lease on life.

We tell God when we fail, but we shouldn't stop there. We need to strive to do better. God forgives us when we ask him to and he gives us the strength to do better next time.

> Finally, brethren, whatever is true, whatever is honor-able, whatever is just, whatever is pure, whatever is lovely, whatever is gracious, if there is any excellence, if there is anything worthy of praise, think about these things. (Philippians 4:8, RSV)

Marty's flicks. Some kids are surprised when we make a new plan instead of accepting excuses for why the old one failed. Marty, a twelve-year-old boy, had missed over half of

47

the first school semester. After working with him through steps one to four, the child said, "I will go to school for the rest of my life." That seemed a little long, so I asked him if part of his life was the next day. He signed a new contract saying that he could make it through the next day, and he would call me that next evening at 7:00 P.M.

At 9:00 P.M. he called and said he was doing fine—until the fifth period. Four kids were looking out the window at the pretty day; and, of course, the teacher was boring, she hated him anyway, and someone suggested "flicking"—leaving school without permission. I didn't even comment on his well-rehearsed monologue of excuses. Almost interrupting him, I asked, "Do you think you can make it through school half a day tomorrow?" Marty called at noon, excited, successful, and ready to make it through the rest of the day.

As a child learns to have faith in himself, he becomes more responsible and achieves greater self-control. Self-control is one of the hardest things for children to learn. One is never an adult until he has learned self-control. Maturity is measured by the amount of self-control a person possesses. The greater the feeling of worth, the greater the self-control.

Christ can renew a child's mind and change his humanistic, sin-debased viewpoint to one dedicated to pleasing God. Certainly it is better to have Christ in control of a child's life, rather than peers, alcohol, or drugs.

STEP EIGHT: DISCIPLINE

Discipline is the eighth step, and it is effective only after the previous seven have been followed. Discipline must be established in the context of relationship (step one). As counselors, we spend 75 percent or more of our time establishing the relationship so that we have the opportunity to spend 25 percent of the time on discipline. Discipline is more effective when the child's model has a real relationship with him; the biological parent is not necessarily an effective model.

The parent or model must be responsible for his own requests. Too often I hear, "My child just won't listen to me. He won't do what I tell him to do." Then when the parent relates what he wants the child to do, I realize I wouldn't do it either. Carefully, without undercutting authority, I help the parent and the child with guidelines.

> The Lord is just in all his ways, and kind in all his doings. (Psalm 145:17, RSV)

Discipline is supposed to give hope; punishment, on the other hand, is intended to force fear. Punishment makes the one doing the punishing feel better; it is intended to hurt the one being punished. Discipline has the intent of a better future; punishment ends with itself. Another of the differences between discipline and punishment is the emotional state of the one doing the punishment.

Jennifer's spill. The table was all set for the important dinner guests. As the little girl was filling the water glasses, the doorbell rang. She was so excited she jumped, knocking a glass of water across the table onto a chair, and then to the floor. The father was ready to wring her neck. That would have been punishment. Instead, he suddenly realized the child's feelings and intent and instead asked her to get a cloth and clean it up. That was appropriate discipline.

Submit yourselves therefore to God. Resist the devil and he will flee from you. (James 4:7, RSV)

Often it takes more grace to discipline than to punish.

A walk in the woods. The mother was hysterical when she called from the hospital. Her son, age fifteen and an only child, had attempted suicide. She was so frightened, she talked too fast. Then she stopped suddenly, and slowly and determinedly said, "Now I want to know how to punish Tom."

I asked her please to wait. She had asked the wrong question. I told her there was a better way. I asked her when was the last time she had seen Tom smile.

It took a while, and then she told of a couple of times when he had smiled after returning from a walk in the woods. Of course, she didn't know what he was doing in the woods.

I took a chance. I asked her to invite her son, if he was able, to walk in the woods with her the next day. Then they were to see me the following day, after the walk.

She was not content with this plan. She felt he needed to be punished. I thought he needed to live.

The boy just stared at his mother when she suggested the walk. Finally he agreed. They walked down one rather familiar path without saying much. Then they stopped under a tree that had snow on its branches. Spontaneously the mother reached up and shook a branch, playfully causing snow to fall on the boy's head.

The boy looked amazed, then smiled. He laughed as he hit her with a snowball. She had almost forgotten how to make one. Her snowball was not the only thing that had missed him by a mile. Until then, so had her methods of parenting.

During the counseling session, I asked Tom what he had to live for. Without hesitation—he smiled slightly, then said, "My mother—she pulled snow down on my head."

The mother learned to discipline. Tom learned to submit. They had fun and laughed together. A relationship was established. They both gained confidence in themselves and in each other.

We have used the following Guidelines for Discipline as a training vehicle at the juvenile court for some time.

1. Discipline is defined as intelligent self-control. The role of the adult in charge is to teach the child that there are certain rules in life that people live by, expecting that the child eventually will adopt these rules for himself. This is working toward a goal of self-discipline.
2. Before establishing limits for the child's behavior, along with him and through him, the adult must determine, as clearly as possible, the ideals, values, and principles by which he lives, and by which he expects the child to live.
3. However, the limits established must not be so constricting that the child does not have the opportunity to manage his own life. The child must have freedom to grow. Starting with the simplest things, such as dressing himself, he must be encouraged to do for himself and take responsibility for his own behavior.
4. Guidelines for setting limits are as follows:
    a. Tell the child clearly what the limitations are. Before you can expect children to do as they are told, you must be sure they understand

right from wrong. You cannot assume they know this distinction unless you tell them, for it involves a learning process. Learning the difference between right and wrong is a slow process. Children have to be told, sometimes shown how and then told all over again, especially in a new situation. The key word is patience.

b. Always go to the child and speak directly to him. Never call him across the room or down the hall. Speak in a quiet, pleasant tone of voice; bend down or kneel so that your face is on a level with his. This way you are sure to have the child's attention while you speak to him.

c. Speak in short, meaningful sentences which the child can understand. Avoid unnecessary explanation.

d. Do not offer a child a choice when you cannot grant a choice. Do not ask, "Would you like to put on your sweater?" If he must do it, say, "It is cold. Please put on your sweater." If you use positive statements, you will not unwittingly offer a child a choice when there is no choice.

e. Suggest or tell in a positive way. "Bounce the ball on the floor." A positive emphasis lets the child know what to do. "Don't hit the window" is a negative approach. It only tells him what not to do. Using positive statements stirs up less resistance in little children. Save the words "don't" and "stop" for those emergencies when it is necessary to put a quick stop to what the child is doing.

Let the children first be fed, for it is not right to take the children's bread. . . . (Mark 7:27, RSV)

Joyce's sin. The fifteen-year-old girl had been the delight of her parents. Joyce was a model student who even studied without being told. A fourteen-year perfect Sunday school attendance pin she had earned was a prize possession to her and her parents. The parents were strong Christians who had only the best aspirations for their daughter. They were also very strict. Yet they did not know good disciplinary principles. Christian education for them had consisted mainly of "thou shalt nots."

It seemed that everything was a sin. Under this style of discipline, the girl was not really internalizing her parents' values, nor was she discovering her own. She was not learning self-discipline. Joyce was not having fun either. She commented several times to me that her parents never smiled.

She knew a sixteen-year-old boy who was really cute—and he had a tremendous line. He asked the naive Joyce if she wanted to go to a party. She knew she shouldn't, but she had heard all the other kids talking about how much fun they were having. She felt guilty as she sneaked out of the house.

She thought the party laughter was loud, even forced. She couldn't remember when she had felt so uncomfortable; yet she was glad to be there.

It wasn't long before the smooth boy sauntered over and asked her if she wanted a joint. Defensively and rather embarrassedly, she softly said, "No." She remembered her parents. "And besides, it is hazardous to your health."

But the boy pushed, "Oh, come on, it's fun."

Joyce did not hesitate; she took a joint and puffed on it. It was not because she did not know better; it was simply that she was not having fun. She had not learned the self-discipline necessary to make a better choice.

Perhaps Joyce's parents would have done better to abide by principles of discipline such as the following:

1. Allow your child to have and accept his feelings while expecting him to control his actions.
2. Reinforce (e.g., praise or reward) behaviors that you want to see continued and/or increased in frequency.
3. Scolding, yelling, and other types of negative attention will often serve to reinforce or increase the frequency of the undesirable behavior.
4. Reinforce every move in the direction of the goal—every improvement in behavior.
5. In the early stage of developing a new behavior in your child, it is important to reinforce every desirable response. Once learning is well under way, the reinforcement should be spaced out.
6. In the long run, ignoring undesirable behavior is often preferable to punishment.
7. Harsh physical punishment should be avoided.
8. Be precise and concrete in placing expectations on your child.
9. Consistency in rules and their enforcement will reduce misbehavior.
10. Never impose rules on your child that you cannot or do not intend to enforce.
11. Provide your child with a positive example of what he should do, not just what he should not do.
12. Learning is facilitated if the child is able to see a

connection between his behavior and the consequences that follow.

13. When possible, reliance upon "natural consequences" is preferable to imposing artificial consequences.

14. Self-control will be facilitated by discussing with the child the reasons behind the rules and limits that are placed on him.

15. Since your child will tend to model or copy you in developing his own set of behaviors, give him a positive model.

16. To teach a child to carry out his responsibilities, require the less preferred activity to come before the more preferred activity.

17. In asking a child to change from an enjoyable behavior to one that is less preferred, allow some time for transition.

18. Using "environmental control" (e.g., "childproofing" your home; providing stimulating activities) minimizes the need for other methods of discipline.

Woe to those who decree iniquitous decrees. (Isaiah 10:1, RSV)

Any discipline employed should be on the same level as the bad behavior which necessitates it. Spanking should be the last resort, after talking and isolation. There is evidence in studies made by child-abuse and victim-assistance professionals that excessive spanking leads to violence. A child should be disciplined only for what he has done—not for the problems of the parents, problems of the economy, or the evil in the world.

Isolation can be an effective means of discipline.

Laura's screams. When my daughter, Laura, was two years old, she would become upset and scream and cry. Fortunately, this did not happen often; but when it did, her mother and I would become very disturbed. One evening she was even more upset than usual. Ann and I were having difficulty coping with the tantrum. Out of frustration and anger, I took Laura to her room, yelled at her, and spanked her.

She merely screamed louder. Her lower lip was quivering; she was hurting. I was hurting.

Cautiously, slowly, I sat on the floor beside her and patted her stiff arm. As she looked at me through her tears, I moved closer and hugged her. "I love you," I whispered. "You may come out of your room when you stop crying."

As I moved to the door, she ran by me, still screaming. I carried her back into her room, looked into her eyes, and whispered firmly, "I love you. When you stop crying, you may come out of your room."

I closed the door. She immediately opened it. I was waiting and whispered my instructions again as I closed the door. After a while she stopped crying. When she came out of her room, we greeted her with much love and praise.

We followed this plan several times until Laura learned to be responsible enough to stop the screaming.

Discipline is far more effective than fear. The present generation of youth does not respond well to threats and fear. You can only scare successful youth into being more successful. You cannot scare failure-oriented youth into success. For instance, you can scare kids who have not taken many drugs out of taking the drugs they are taking. But seldom can you scare a kid who really is hooked on drugs out of it completely.

While I was working in a reformatory, we had seminars for high school kids to try to scare them "straight." The inmates got into fights over who could tell the "worst rap." I'm not sure the kids were very impressed.

No kid in a thousand really believes he is going to get caught. Even when he sees a peer in trouble, he just thinks, "That's tough, but it will never happen to me. I'm too smart."

Most of the youth referred to the court were raised at one end of the discipline spectrum or the other. Either the parents were very strict or very lenient.

It seems to me that children often have a natural desire to please their parents. Certainly problems occur when this desire is frustrated; bad behavior results. But how we choose to discipline really matters.

Fear does not last. Love does. Salvation is not based upon the wrath of God, but rather on the love of God.

> Return, O Israel, to the Lord your God, for you have stumbled because of your iniquity. (Hosea 14:1, RSV)

Effective discipline also means permitting natural consequences to occur. A child stumbles because of his own iniquity. We want to protect our children, but we must realize that they also learn from their own bad experiences. Each child is an individual, and so decisions concerning discipline must be made individually.

If a child has some control over the consequences, then it is discipline and not punishment.

Gary's decision. It was Gary's senior year and he ranked high academically in his class. But he refused to take gym.

He was a pleasant youth. We discussed his athletic ability in which he achieved average performance. He liked to play most sports, particularly baseball. He was about six feet tall and of average weight. We discussed many reasons why a youth would not want to take gym or showers, and he assured me that he was "normal" in every way. He said he just did not want to go.

He never did tell me what was really going on or why he had this fear. But he made a choice: he did not graduate.

He took gym the next year and graduated a year late. He knew the consequences and was willing to accept them. His parents were willing for him to do as he wished, and they continued to provide support for him for an extra year. Such was his life and theirs.

God also disciplines, but I don't believe he "punishes." I think the theology of testing is overstated. Natural consequences happen, and we suffer. God also suffers. Yet he promises strength anyway. He blesses us with love, joy, peace, patience, kindness, generosity, and faith.

Sometimes God disciplines by isolation. Adam and Eve were thrown out of the Garden of Eden. The Israelites went through their exile. Hell is separation from God. Man's actions make hell the natural consequence of his behavior—thus we bring punishment on ourselves.

Nowhere in Scripture does it say that the righteous are spared all difficulties and trials. Likewise, the wicked do not always receive immediate punishment or trouble. Yet the rewards of the righteous even in the midst of troubles can be love, joy, peace, patience, endurance, kindness, generosity, faith, mildness, and charity (see Galatians 5:22, 23). The results of materialism are: lewd conduct, idolatry, sorcery, hostility, bickering, jealousy, selfish rivalry, fractions, drunkenness, and the like.

STEP NINE: NEVER GIVE UP

The entire "theology of hope" has practical meaning in this final step toward a better life. Jesus promises that he will never leave us without comfort; he will come to us. God gives more grace when the burden grows greater. As Isaiah said, "Those who hope in God shall never be disappointed." We fail; but God is there to pick us up again and again.

We must never give up on our child. We must always pray and "keep on keeping on." The alternative to maintaining our hope is falling into despair.

God's grace is sufficient for us. But we need to pray for patience and long-suffering with our children. We never know when the moment will arrive that the child becomes teachable. One of the most important factors in dealing with children, particularly children in crisis, is to be able to tell when that teachable moment arises. It is sheer tragedy to give up too soon and miss the opportunity for a constructive change. In too many cases, because of our own time commitments or frustrations, we give up.

Sometimes it takes years to change a child's behavior pattern. If a child is seventeen years of age, he may have spent years learning his present behavior pattern. He has had time to build up a strong wall of distrust of others. If we expect that the wall will be broken in a few months, we make a serious mistake. Our expectations are too high. At times it will take a year or longer just to accomplish step one.

Our feeling of success or failure will be determined by how we feel about what we have done with the child. Our success is based upon what we have or have not done— not upon what the child has or has not done.

We must not give up even if the child does not tell us his problems. We need to wait until the child himself is ready to trust us. We don't say, "Let's talk about your problems"; instead, we say, "Let's go out and get a hamburger," or "Let's go do something together."

Never giving up really means waiting for the child. We must not be the type of parent whose message is that we are too busy, or that we are not really listening. We must have patience, love, and a willingness to stick it out, no matter how long it takes. We must be willing to communicate and to care, even when the child himself has given up. By our concern, if by no other factor, we will eventually get his attention.

> But Jesus said, "Let the children come to me, and do not hinder them; for to such belongs the kingdom of heaven." (Matthew 19:14, RSV)

When we allow the child to fail as the natural consequences of his actions, we have not let him down. There are even times, desperate times, when parents must lock an older child out or ask him to leave. However, the parent still prays and continues to hope for recovery and healing.

First words. A mother called and wanted me to do something—anything—with her son. She had tried "everything" and the eight-year-old still would not do what she wanted. She said she had given up, and she was also ready to give up on his little sister.

The mother brought the eight-year-old into the office. He had not been going to school and had many other problems. The mother also brought the little sister, two and a half years old. She sat the little girl down on a chair and pushed her back so her legs were straight out. The mother said, "Sit there, and don't you move!"

In seeming anguish the mother started telling me how terrible her little boy was. I noticed that after about fifteen minutes the little girl slowly moved up from the back of the chair and dropped her legs down. The mother screamed, "I told you not to move! I am going to put that trash can on your head."

I had my own idea about another placement of the trash can.

I quickly moved over to the little girl, who had not looked up until I spoke to her. Then I could see hurt that I seldom see even in the eyes of a sixteen-year-old.

I keep candy in my desk drawer. I took some candy and knelt in front of the little girl, trying to attain direct eye contact.

I asked her if she wanted a piece of candy. She looked at her mother for permission. I gave her the candy and said, "Thank you," a couple of times. Then her mother asked if I was expecting the child to say, "Thank you." I said, "Sure." The mother emphatically replied, "Well, she has never spoken a word in her life. I gave up long ago trying to get her to talk."

At that point I softly said to the little boy, "Have you ever said anything good to your mother?" Going on, I asked, "Have you ever thanked your mother for the food she cooks? Do you think it would be possible this week to say something good about your mother's cooking?" He agreed. I told him that the more good things he said to his mother, the better off she would be. Of course, I was really talking indirectly to the mother, but could not give this advice to her. She was too defensive.

The next week the little boy was so excited as he related how he had told his mother the night before that she cooked "good." He added, with a gleam in his eye and his tongue halfway out, "And it was liver. Yuk!" Then he almost yelled, "And do you know what? Last night she put me to bed and she kissed me!"

As he was talking, I noticed that the little girl was walking around her brother. She put her hand on my desk drawer. I asked if she wanted candy. I know about sugar, nutrition, and hyperactive kids, but there was another priority here. I invited the mother and boy to leave the office. I sat the darling child on my lap and let her draw all over my blotter while eating her candy. As she drew, I kept praising her. The mother came back in and accused me of ruining the little girl's dinner. Better to ruin her dinner than ruin her life.

They left, but in a moment the little girl stepped back to the door. She raised her hand and waved. I bent down in front of her. I noticed that two of her fingers were stuck together. Suddenly she whispered, "Thank you." Her first words!

3
QUALITIES OF CARING PARENTS

The nine steps in the previous chapters specifically outline relationship and trust building for the purpose of rearing responsible children. Generally there are four qualities which are always necessary in a caring parent. Love, faith, fun, and hope must be demonstrated prayerfully to a child, with the added objective that the child will also internalize these qualities.

> I am the vine, you are the branches. He who abides in me, and I in him, he it is that bears much fruit, for apart from me you can do nothing. (John 15:5, RSV)

As we abide in Christ we daily seek to pass this abiding strength on to our children. The secret to abiding is love. Thus the first quality for a parent is to demonstrate love.

Laura's bike. When our daughter Laura was six, she informed me that it was time to take the training wheels off her bicycle. I knew she could not ride without the training wheels, but she was eager to try. I held onto the handle bars and the back of the seat as she went wobbling down the driveway.

Finally, as she gained speed, I could hold on no longer. It was so difficult to let go. I knew she would crash, but I let go and prayed, "God, let it not hurt too much."

When she crashed, I quickly picked up my little girl and put her back on the bike, brushing away her tears. "We'll make it together," I told her.

As we started up the driveway, Laura said, "Daddy, you're holding on too tight."

"Laura, I want to catch you when you fall."

"Daddy, catch me when I fall, but please stop catching me before I fall!"

It is difficult to be a good parent. A parent must decide several times a day when to hold on and when to let go even a little. We know that our children will fall and hurt themselves, but we also know that with God's guidance we can pick them up and put them back on life's way.

We want to hold our children close, guide them, and pray that they will become responsible adults themselves. If we hold on too tightly they might become dependent upon us for the rest of our lives. If we let go gradually, they have a better chance of becoming responsible adults. Even though we must give up our children physically, there should never be a time when we give them up spiritually.

We need to feel the presence of the Holy Spirit in our daily lives as we seek our Lord's guidance as parents. We must apply our theology in everyday situations with our children. Our Christianity does not automatically make us good parents; however, biblical thinking is the vital first step.

Children must be loved and accepted for who they are now—not because of what they have or have not done in the past, or what they will or will not do in the future. We accept our children because they are our children. Sometimes this is difficult because of their unruly behavior. The behavior is not acceptable—but they are. Nonacceptance can lead to worse behavior in both parents and children. But children's self-image improves, they increase in strength and are enabled to improve their behavior.

Good behavior should be maximized; bad behavior should be minimized. Bad behavior must not be ignored, but neither should it be stressed. As parents, we want our children to be aware of our negative reactions, but we do not want them or ourselves to be overcome by negatives. We must emphasize positive reactions.

> So faith, hope, love abide, these three; but the greatest of these is love. (1 Corinthians 13:13, RSV)

Well-done eggs. Responsible youth are able to show love. A mother pushed her fourteen-year-old son into my office and commanded him, "You sit there." Then she pointed her finger at me and ordered, "You fix him."

I did not know exactly what she meant. Then she began relating all the bad things her son had done, while the youth stared at the floor.

She gave me two pieces of paper which listed the child's behavior and academic achievements. At the top of one sheet was the name "Tom." This paper showed that Tom was failing every class.

At the top of the second paper was the name "Tommy," and this paper indicated that he was beating up every kid in the school.

I could have responded in many ways. I could have said firmly, "Listen, kid, you are going to have to study hard or you will not make it through high school, and certainly not college." But it wouldn't have helped because he was not goal-oriented.

I could have warned, "You'd better be careful or you will get slugged in the mouth." But his masculine ego was at stake and I knew that neither approach would work.

Remembering his two names, I asked him, "What do you want me to call you?" He sat and stared at me and I back at him. We both waited silently.

Finally he asked, "Are you a preacher man?"

I smiled and said, "Yes, I am," waving my cross to emphasize it.

He frowned, "Well, then, don't call me nothing."

I asked, "Is there anything you can do well?"

He smiled, "Yes, I do something good; I'm good with chicks."

He turned to his mother, saying, "Hey, Mom, how about leavin' me alone with the preacher man for a while?"

When his mother left, he said, "See how small I am, preacher? I'm small and I ain't got no father."

He continued to talk for several minutes, then mentioned his mother.

I asked how they got along.

He scowled, "Fine, just fine!"

I asked, "Would you like to get along better with your mother?"

After some thought he answered, "Yeah, I would." This was a very important decision; he had to choose to make an effort.

I quizzed, "What can you do to get along better with your mother?"

He said, "My mama can stop screaming at me."

I said, "Wait a minute. I want to know what you are going to do."

The responsibility for change in a child's life does not belong only to the parent, school, or church. Depending upon age, responsibility for change must be heavily placed upon the child.

Tom said, "I can't think of anything I can do." He folded his arms and chirped, "I'm perfect."

I said, "Do you think that during this week you can think of two kind things to say to your mother?"

Tom said, "Maybe, I can try, I guess."

The goal had to be simple and achievable. He had to build his life into a success, not a failure. We would have gained nothing if he had come back having failed, or had not come back at all. I asked if he could agree to do one kind thing. He said he could. So we wrote a contract, signed by both of us, to be taped in a conspicuous place in his room.

I asked if he loved his mother. It took a while, but he finally was able to admit he did.

The next week he came running into my office excitedly, shouting, "Preacher man, I made my mother cry!" I knew he had done this many times before. He continued, "I came downstairs and put my arms around my mother and asked, 'Mama, did you have a good night's sleep?'"

It was a kind thing to ask. His mother was startled. He was having so much fun, he offered to fix breakfast.

He reminded me of how often I had told him to be positive. He said that, positively, he had gotten half of an egg in the pan. As he was "trying to push the egg around in the pan," he told his mother he loved her. Then he smiled, "Preacher man, you should have heard those tears."

I responded that this was fine, but I did not know one could hear tears.

"You don't know my mama," he insisted.

They had sat down and had a blessing before the meal for the first time in his life. They thanked God for the "well-done eggs," as his mother called them—they were actually praying about themselves.

The boy continued to be kind and the mother stopped screaming. He was building faith in himself and in God.

After a month, he was fixing mushroom omelettes and they were having longer blessings.

LOVE

> For God so loved the world, that he gave his only begotten Son, that whosoever believeth in him should not perish, but have everlasting life. (John 3:16, KJV)

We demonstrate to our children by our actions that we love them.

Fetch-It-Freddy. "Captain Kangaroo" was one of my favorite television programs. When Ann, my wife, was teaching school, I had the responsibility of getting our children ready in the mornings.

"Captain Kangaroo" gave our morning a structure. We knew that by the first television commercial, breakfast had to be eaten; by the second, teeth brushed; and by the third, shoes on. At 8:30, we had to go out the door. The timing worked for me as well as my children.

One commercial began by showing in the background a man reading behind a newspaper. Only his legs were visible. The camera quickly focused upon two darling children who were playing with a small plastic dog. The commercial announced something to the effect that Fetch-It-Freddy would catch any ball rolled to it, as we saw.

Children rolled the ball, and Fetch-It-Freddy would catch it. Then a large ball rolled across the floor and hit Fetch-It-Freddy. The little girls looked around, and with delight upon their faces, exclaimed, "Wow, Daddy!"

Daddy got down on the floor and put his arms around the children and hugged them. The theme seemed to be, "You too can have fun together with Fetch-It-Freddy."

As a Santa Claus helper, I went to different stores that Christmas and discovered that Fetch-It-Freddy was one of the hottest items of the year. Many children apparently thought that if they had a Fetch-It-Freddy, their daddies might become more than newspapers with legs, and would get down on the floor and play with them.

The quality of the time spent with our children is more important than the quantity. Children must sense that we genuinely want to spend time with them. Some elderly parents are lonely today because they let their children be lonely when they were teenagers. Unless we demonstrate our love by our behavior, our children are not going to believe our words.

Most youth detained in the juvenile court of Summit County describe parents who never got down on the floor and played with them. The same youth also responded that they do not feel their parents love them at all. Love is getting down, hugging, and playing with our children. The gospel message is that God sent Jesus down into the world to be close to us and to give us salvation. The person of Jesus Christ reveals to us that God loves us and wants to be near us. His love is always with our children, no matter how unlovable they seem to be. His care sustains them even when we cannot. In order to learn to be competent, children must know that we love them and that God loves them.

Often I sense the loneliness of children. For them, discovering the truth of God's love and presence is crucial.

Trina's doll. Children are stronger when they are able to give and to receive love. My little daughter has a doll that squeaks, "I love you." It also asks, "Do you love me?" My daughter loves this doll and all the other thirty-some dolls and stuffed creatures in her room. Children need not only to be loved, but also to love. Pets can help meet this need. But most importantly, children need parents to love.

FAITH

> Now faith is the assurance of things hoped for, the conviction of things not seen. (Hebrews 11:1, RSV)

Faith is the second attribute for parents to exemplify in the rearing of responsible children. A child must have faith in himself and in God in order to feel and to be successfully motivated.

House burglar. As a child gains faith in himself, he also internalizes a feeling of worth. Bill, a child in detention, told me of the seventeen homes he had broken into during the previous month. He seemed sincere in his desire to stop this delinquent behavior, but apparently did not have the strength to do so.

I visited him at his request. When I walked into his room, he said, "Hey, chaplain, will you pray for me?"

I answered, "I'll pray with you."

"Well," he said, "I've never prayed before."

"Well, now's a good time to start. Go ahead. Pray as you feel you can."

Bill closed his eyes and prayed, "God, do I feel terrible." I reminded him of his desire to change his behavior. He continued, "God, help me not to break into any more houses as long as I live." I added, "Especially not tomorrow after he gets out."

He made a commitment to call me the next evening. He was very excited when he called. He had left the detention home, and the next day he was leisurely walking along with tape and glass cutters in his pocket when he saw his neighbors drive away. He sneaked up to the back door, but just as he started to tape the glass, he remembered his prayer and his commitment and ran home to call me.

Each morning for over six months now he has prayed, "God, help me to have a good day, and God, help me not to break into houses." Good boy. Great God!

Faith in God promotes faith in self. The child must believe that when God sent his Son into the world, he bought us with a price, the precious blood of the Lord Jesus Christ. Therefore, we are worth something.

Faith in God makes a difference. Only 6 percent of the youth referred to the Summit County Juvenile Court have attended church once in the previous two years. I am not sure all those who say they have attended actually have: A boy told me he attends church almost every Sunday but he gets tired of the same song, "Silent Night."

A child and parent must be saved from the sins of the world and their own sins. They can be saved by believing upon the Lord Jesus Christ, confessing their sins, and daily praying for the blessing of abundant life. "The family that prays together stays together" most generally rings true. Individual and family devotions encourage the attitude of getting to know God, of receiving guidance, of taking needs to God, and of fortifying the family structure.

A seventeen-year-old wrestler lifted weights daily to prepare for the big events. He said he also read his Bible, memorized verses, and prayed as a way of exercising in preparation for future big events. He learned to wait upon the Lord, and his strength was renewed.

Faith comes by hearing the Word of God. Children need to be aware that when they lack wisdom they can ask of God. A child, just like an adult, is saved from his sins by following the plan of salvation.

First the child recognizes God's love as revealed in Jesus Christ. Second, the child acknowledges that what he is doing is not good. Third, the child considers his life, and decides he is in "big trouble." Fourth, he repents, asks forgiveness, and decides he wants to do better. Fifth, he accepts the gift of God, of eternal life through Jesus Christ.

> When we cry, "Abba! Father!" it is the Spirit himself bearing witness with our spirit that we are children of God. (Romans 8:15, 16, RSV)

My faith. My own faith in God developed gradually through a process of warm feelings and cold doubts. During my childhood I was aware of God's love and the love of my parents, Wenrich and Mildred Arledge. My first religious experience occurred one Sunday morning. I could not find my shoes, a frequent experience. I prayed and I found them.

A true relationship with God started to develop during my sophomore year of college. It began when I took a girl whom I had eagerly waited to date to a seminar on religion at Ohio State University, three hours from my college in Georgetown, Kentucky. I discussed my faith with her as we drove, and things were going great.

The first speaker that night was a beautiful young woman from Japan who lectured about the Shinto faith. I decided that I could probably agree with almost everything she said. She showed the audience the callused knees she had from crawling up the state shrine steps, and I was impressed. She was sincere as she emphasized nationalism and being good to her neighbor. Since I had been involved in debate and speech contests, I rated her according to public speaking points. I smilingly told my date that the speaker had done quite well. My date frowned, "She wasn't so good." At that moment I think someone turned on the air conditioning!

The second speaker was a young man from India who demonstrated the lotus position as part of the practice of his Hindu faith. He advocated applying the spiritual principles of his religion to the social and political sphere. He emphasized moral growth that is a mystic union with ultimate reality. He seemed so sure that integral yoga would enable a man to become a superman. When I commented to my date that he was pretty good, she just stared at me, and I wondered why the blower was turned up on the air conditioning!

Third, a girl from Chile very nervously presented her faith in the Lord Jesus Christ. With great difficulty, she stammered around until she sat down in less than three minutes. "Wow, she was having difficulty," I volunteered. "She was great," my date asserted, and I felt put down.

The last speaker was a handsome young man from the Near East who rather emotionally gave his personal testimony of what Allah had done for him. This Muslim spoke of the prophet Mohammed as though he were a personal friend. He concluded by giving praise to Allah, saying that it was an answer to the prayers of many people that he was in America studying at Ohio State. I think if we had sung,

"Just As I Am," I might have gone forward, this man was so convincing!

I could not help but comment upon the four presentations, saying that the last was best. My date shook her head, bit her lip, and said loudly, "The girl from Chile was the best. She was the Christian. The Christians always win." I was going to debate that with her, but thought we would probably be interrupted by announcement of an upcoming blizzard!

As we drove back to Georgetown College that evening, I had plenty of time to think while my date very, very silently hung onto her door handle. I wondered why I believed in God anyway. Certainly, I thought, if I had been raised in the Near East I would believe in Allah. Was my religion my own or was it a product of my Christian parents, or even the result of living in a "Christian nation?"

The next three evenings I prayed over and over, "God, make yourself known to me." All I experienced was the "O holy silence." I prayed more earnestly, even on my knees. Nothing! After a week, I finally challenged, "All right, God, you made the waters divide; you can move mountains. I want you to move the curtain in my room just a little bit. Make yourself known to me." Still nothing! The "O holy" unmoving curtain.

I had not been feeling well during that semester, so I kept praying that God would make me better. I did not. To make matters worse, there was a kid living in my hall whom I knew was a real sinner. Once, while I spent a late evening moment in intense prayer, the guy knocked on my door and then barged in to tell me excitedly about his evening. He was ecstatic. It was not fair. The way he was sinning, he should have been struck sick—really sick. I cautiously prayed, "OK, God, if you can't make me feel better, at least make that sinner sick." The next day I felt bad and the sinner looked healthier than a horse!

Between classes I yelled at God. Nothing! In desperation that night I very quietly asked for God, "You there, Whomever," to become real to me. Still nothing!

Oh, how I wanted a car! Typical of guys my age. I looked out my window and saw an open parking place. I confidently prayed to "Whomever" that a car would appear in that spot. I continued to pray for over an hour, when, sure enough, a car pulled into the spot. I became more depressed to see my neighboring sinner leap out of the car—with one of the prettiest girls on campus. Forget it. There could not be a God.

The next day I skipped my classes. I was sick. But somehow I calmly began to pray again. Then I saw my dusty Bible. I took it, closed my eyes, and opened it to wherever. With eyes still closed, I circled around the verses with my finger. I stopped upon Romans 8:16. As I read the verse the very Spirit of God bore witness to my troubled spirit. Something happened. I felt alive; I felt real; I felt calm. I knew that God had made himself known to me. I looked immediately at the curtain. It still did not move. I looked out the window for my car. Not there. I evaluated whether I felt physically better. I did not. But what I did feel was so powerful that the curtain did not need to move. The car did not need to appear. My stomach did not need to feel better. God was there.

My theology. The basis for my theology is revealed in the last portion of Matthew 25: "When I was in prison, you came to visit me."

While seeing over 2,000 youth a year at the Summit County Juvenile Court Center and the Protestant Youth Counseling Service, I often wish I could change the families

77

of these children, motivate them in school, or work with them every day. But the Scripture verse does not say, "I was in prison and you came and changed my life," or, "I was in prison and you got me a job," or, "I was in prison and you changed my mother."

One of the hardest lessons for me to learn is the limitations of particular situations. Many youth I see only one time. How frustrating! But I can "visit" that child. I can assess the child and his situation, then quickly begin to establish a relationship. My constant prayer is, "God, help me make them smile." Then I wait and watch eagerly until God's miracle of relationship begins.

Even the slightest effort a child makes in seeking strength to change is exciting. Then we both smile and draw closer together. Matthew 25 promises that our visits will bring blessings from the Father, who created all children with the potential for smiling. The smile is the beginning of a long process toward responsibility—and, hopefully, a Christian life.

> And if you be unwilling to serve the Lord, choose this day whom you will serve, whether the gods your fathers served in the region beyond the River, or the gods of the Amorites in whose land you dwell; but as for me and my house, we will serve the Lord. (Joshua 24:15, RSV)

As parents we must decide we are going to serve the Lord in rearing our children. Our Christianity does not automatically make us good parents, but it is a vital first step. It takes more of God's strength to praise our children than to scream at them. In order for a child to have faith in himself, we must praise him. Often parents tell me they can find nothing in their child to praise, for they—the parents—are too angry.

The kid with the shoes. Appropriate discipline follows praise.

A seventeen-year-old boy walked slowly into my office with his arms folded. Slouching down in the chair seemingly added to his defense. Even though his lips were tightly pressed, I could hear him grinding his teeth. He knew I had a police report concerning his shoplifting charge of the previous weekend, and he was well aware that I had talked with his school counselor concerning his constant fighting. Further, the grinding grew louder as he thought of what his father might have disclosed in a telephone call.

The child was ready for me. He had the "look" that nothing was going to touch him. I smiled. I usually smile at a youth who comes into the office, particularly if one is ready to fight. The smile caught him off guard. I knew in order to get through to the child at all, I had to find something, anything, to praise him for. I ended the silence with, "I see you tied your left shoe."

It seemed like such an inappropriate remark. He looked surprised, then agreed. "Yeah, yeah, yeah." He was not ready for praise, and it must have been the first time in a long while anyone had praised him for anything. In fact, he later remarked about this. I knew that if I did not establish a positive relationship with him, talking about the negative reports would not make any difference anyway.

The boy had to have faith in himself. He had to have faith that he had done something right—anything. He smiled back, hesitantly at first, then boldly, "Look, I tied both of them," he called to my attention. "I have a pair of black loafers," he volunteered. "I don't tie them."

79

The smiles progressed to chuckles—almost laughter—as he back-stepped verbally through many shoes, even to the bronzed ones on his mother's mantel. After about ten minutes the rapport was a "shoe-in," and we could talk. Slowly, he said, "This has been a rough week." He told me about his behavior. I agreed. We were able to discuss it and to take appropriate disciplinary action.

In order to instill within our children faith in themselves, we must first praise them. If we want children to do right, we must tell them over and over again of the right they already do, and then they will do more and more right. But if we remind them over and over of the wrong they do, they will do more and more wrong. What a difference!

Every day we must find something for which we can hug our child and proclaim, "You did it!" We need to encourage our children to feel a sense of accomplishment. Make them smile!

Eagerly catch them in your arms as they reach up to you, loudly proclaiming, "I did it!" No matter what else happens around them, no matter what negative things, no matter what anyone else does—our children can be satisfied for a moment that they "did it." Then they can develop faith in themselves. As we put our children to bed each night, they should be able to tell us of at least one thing they did well. If they cannot, they have not failed alone. We too have failed to provide an environment conducive to success.

"An 'atta boy' response works better than a 'you dummy,'" is a slogan of Father Paul F. Selle, the Catholic chaplain at the Juvenile Court Center. An "atta boy" could consist of a pat on the back, even a smile of approval. A "you dummy" is a negative response—for instance, when a child receives four Ds and one C on his report card and the parent screams, "Four Ds! If you don't study you will be in that grade for six years! You are grounded." After this the child will probably do worse and make Fs the next time.

Instead, with a silent prayer and an "atta boy" attitude, parents should look again and say, "Oh, you got a C. Wonderful." The child will probably go into shock.

Start together to discuss the subject in which the child has done well. When the child can stand it no longer and finally says, "I have other subjects," our chance has arrived. Calmly we ask, "What can we do together about these other subjects?"

We can always express our feelings, but it is our behavior that makes the difference.

A parent must draw on the strength of God to invite children to go bowling, when at the time he wants to preach against drugs. After a "bowling relationship" has been established, then he can discuss drugs. Sometimes it takes God's strength to be silent. Children will grow strong through praise, but they become weak and delinquent through ridicule. Praise your child even if you must search for something to praise. It is through praise that a good relationship is built.

> Train up a child in the way he should go; and when he is old he will not depart from it. (Proverbs 22:6, RSV)

Children gain faith in themselves after feeling the sense of success. Success grows through learning responsibility. Responsibility is not something that appears overnight; it is gradually learned. It is not a gift that can be bestowed; it is earned.

Charlie's Corvette. Charlie was promised a Corvette when he graduated from high school. He was eagerly looking

81

forward to the car, but he did not pass a single class, and therefore did not graduate. His wealthy father gave him the Corvette anyway.

Two weeks later the father called me, extremely distressed, because Charlie had totaled the car, broken his arm, and suffered other minor injuries. The father expressed this frustration: "I don't know what to do with him. I just can't understand it." I do not know how the father could have expected the child to have any responsibility over the Corvette when Charlie had shown no responsibility over his grades.

Parents sometimes take too much responsibility for their children. Then, curiously enough, when the child fails the parent becomes the "bad guy." When a sixteen-year-old tells his father he wants a car, the typical response of most parents is, "You've got to be nuts." Instead, we should smile and say, "Sure, son," as we pat him on the back, "you may have a car." The boy might casually ask, as the family is eating dinner, "Will you pass the potatoes, and when do I get my car?" Then you should smile, silently pray, and say, "Here are the potatoes, and I don't know. When are you going to get your car? When are you going to earn the money for the expense of buying and operating your car?" Then the responsibility is upon the child to work for the car. And once the child has earned it, he will appreciate it.

One youth, seventeen years old, had carried papers, mowed lawns, and done whatever else he could do to earn enough money to buy a moped. He rode the moped to his counseling sessions with me. When I asked if I might ride it, I was told to buy my own, just as he tells anyone else who asks!

The successful completion of tasks through responsible behavior excites our children, makes them feel good, and makes them smile. How good it is to have accomplished something. How sad it is not to have anything to be proud of.

A mother brought her son to my office to complain because he had "failed" and missed half the table when he dusted. She failed first because she did not praise the responsible behavior that the four-year-old displayed in dusting at all; and second, she failed because she did not praise him for the half that he dusted!

We should train up a child in the way the Lord has created him to go, not so much the way the parent wants him to. Then when he is old he will not depart from the Lord. A positive self-image is a product of relationship to God as well as a positive family relationship.

> For the Lord is good; his steadfast love endures for ever, and his faithfulness to all generations. (Psalm 100:5, RSV)

As our children gain strength from faith in their capabilities, they prepare themselves to accept responsibility. The cyclic process works as follows: Children's successful completion of tasks through responsible behavior leads to increased faith in themselves, which leads to increased success. As parents, we should begin from birth to reveal to our children their own abilities, so that responsibility will be developed simply as part of their character. Responsibility can be given, expected, and earned. It should not be forced upon a child; but rather, the child must be gradually led into it. Children must learn to take responsibility for their own behavior.

Five-stance quo. Mark's fist slammed against my office door as he ducked his six-foot-five frame to enter. He had not waited for me to greet him in my waiting room. His right hand rested upon my desk as he grabbed the back of my chair, slowly leaned over me, and angrily announced, "I have been ordered to come see you; I fight!" I could have responded in many traditional ways. Instead, I smiled and said, "You like to fight?"

"Yeah, man." He spent about ten minutes relating in detail his bloody conquests, his excitement when a tooth goes through a lip. He informed me that his performance level was higher than his verbal level. With a "come on" motion he requested that I stand up.

God blessed me with a few brains; I remained seated. He was disappointed and I had his attention.

I asked if he had a better life because he fought. He looked as if the question clearly disturbed him. I heard him mutter three times, "Yeah, man." He proudly related that when he walked through the halls all the boys moved out of his way. All the girls smiled. He was king.

The session was over. He asked, to my surprise, if he could come back.

The next Thursday, he came bounding into my office. He was excited to show me his new fight pattern, "the five-stance quo." He stood with his feet perpendicular and his left arm extended far, with fingers tight. His right hand was drawn under his chin. He lowered his head, displaying the "killer" look. He had worked hard on "the look." Somehow he was not confident in his demonstration speech. He asked me to help him by standing up.

Surprise! I remained seated.

He sat down. I asked what he could do if he ever wanted to do anything else besides fighting. Nothing. I could not interest him in sports. To him, "making some dude bleed" is a sport. He, of course, did not have any intention of being involved with school, home, or church. He did not even care to be involved with girls. I knew we were in trouble.

Silence fell over the session. Finally, he asked who could help him stop fighting even if he wanted to. He stood tall, looked down at me, and giggled, "Would you?" I pointed up.

"What's that?" he demanded.

"God."

"Who?"

He thought God was only a swear word. I told him God was a person who could help him. He stood in his favorite "five-stance quo" and informed me, with emphasis, "There ain't no God, never was, and never will be!" He growled as he instructed, "God is for punks who don't know the five-stance quo."

I looked up to heaven, stood up (behind my chair), pointed, and testified, "There is a God, always has been, and always will be; and God can help you to stop fighting!" He growled louder, punched the air, and stormed out of the office. My heart sank; I had lost another kid.

The first Monday client was a small thirteen-year-old who was just beginning to relate to me some real problems, when, without a knock, the door was abruptly thrown open. Mark entered the office, pressed his fist against the child's nose, told him, "You don't have any problems. Get out!" I asked the younger child to go to the waiting room.

Mark stared at the floor. He looked different—much different. Softly and slowly he began to talk. He had been so angry when he left the office the previous Thursday that he could think only of the many things he wanted to do with my head; no one had ever stood up to him before.

He aimlessly and recklessly drove around. As he was stopped at a light, a "wimp" (Mark's term) pulled up beside him, rolled down his window, and shouted something derogatory about Mark's mother.

Mark was familiar with the terminology, having used it many times before himself. Curiously, he did not shout back the usual response, but instead pointed toward a Red Barn restaurant parking lot.

The challenger laid rubber and squealed into the lot. Some kids ran out of the Red Barn and others got out of the front and back seats of cars. It was time for action.

Slowly Mark drove into the lot. He stopped the car, taking time to turn off the motor. Slowly he opened the door and let his left leg slide out of the car. Almost gracefully he let his right foot rest on the pavement. With a sense of fitness he stood to tower over his five-foot-eight challenger, who quickly cleared his throat and admitted, "It must have been somebody else's mother."

This far from satisfied Mark as he grabbed the boy's throat, threw him against the car, got into the five-stance quo position and prepared to knock the boy's teeth out.

Then something happened. Mark felt something he had never felt before. He told me that he looked down and for the first time really saw a boy not just as a "thing with teeth." Mark said he looked into the boy's eyes and saw fear; he looked into his mouth and saw braces.

Mark commented to the boy on the braces. The challenger's tongue secured his teeth. He cautiously moved his hand to point to his mouth. Talking as well as he could with Mark's grip around his neck, the boy uttered, "Dad's paying a lot of money for these."

Mark's previous feeling was gone. He tightened his grip and shouted, "I don't care. I'm still going to knock your teeth out." Miraculously, the previous feeling returned and Mark recognized the Lord's presence. He told the boy that God was telling him not to knock his teeth out. Almost in shock, the boy felt for his teeth, wiggled his neck, and testified, "I believeth in Godeth." Mark loosened his command and ordered the "challenger" to go and act like it.

The news was out. Mark wasn't fighting anymore. First thing Friday morning, three boys tried to goad him into a fight. By noon seven boys and two girls had attempted to claim the "king" title. By Monday afternoon, twenty-two would-be contenders were active in threats. Mark was not fighting. Mark was chanting, over and over, "For the Lord is good; his steadfast love endures forever. Lord, help me not to fight. Help me to study instead." As Mark related his chant, he smiled.

I was the only one who came for Mark at his graduation. Others stood and cheered with pride when their beloved received his certificate of success. When Mark received his, he looked around and saw me standing in his favorite pose, the five-stance quo. We cheered. The Lord was faithful.

FUN

> Or what man of you, if his son asks him for bread, will give him a stone? (Matthew 7:9, RSV)

Picnic wishing. Fun is the third guideline for rearing responsible children. Loving parents are warm, not cold as stone.

Father Selle once asked a sixteen-year-old boy, "If you could have anything in the world, what would you like to have?" He expected to hear "a new Corvette," "a million dollars"—the usual things.

The boy thought for a long time and then very quietly and seriously answered, "I would like to go on a picnic with my family—my mother, my father, and my brothers and sisters."

His parents had been divorced and he had not seen one brother in a long time.

He continued, "We would not need to go very far or be gone very long. We would not even have to take chicken. Just so we could all be together."

It is very apparent to me that families of troubled youth usually do not spend time having fun together.

Father Selle and I sometimes were called the "detention home tormentors." I think one of our main missions has been to tease the detained children. We learned never to ridicule or put them down. At first, they were amazed. We would get a special enjoyment after "teasing" a hostile child for a couple of days, then watching the corners of his mouth slowly turn up as we would see his first smile. After the smile, he usually was ready to talk.

I stress again that we must learn to have fun with our children. This idea is commonly expressed by the word "fun," and bibically by the word "joy." In church groups it is often called "fellowship." My experiences of being with people in mental hospitals, in a reformatory, and the past eleven years at the Juvenile Court Center, have convinced me that the cause of most of our problems is our tendency to grasp at pleasure and instant gratification without achieving a sense of satisfaction.

The majority of the children referred to the juvenile court do not know how to have fun. Most were not involved in any organized sports activity or "sand lot sports" when they were first referred to the court. Few of these delinquent youth were reared with an emphasis upon family fun and involvement. They need to learn to have fun.

> I the Lord search the mind and try the heart, to give to every man according to his ways, according to the fruit of his doings. (Jeremiah 17:10, RSV)

Talented child. All youth must learn the art of having fun.

An extremely talented child went from his high school to a university for additional classes. During a special program he was awarded two trophies. He walked from the assembly to his car, opened the trunk, put the trophies inside, and for no apparent reason, removed a tire iron.

Before the security police could wrestle him to the ground, he had smashed the windshields of seven cars. The child was absolutely shocked at his own actions. The parents, in stunned disbelief, asked repeatedly, "Why?"

As I talked with him, I discovered that many people loved him, that he had great faith in himself and was very creative. He was also religious and was a leader in his church youth group.

I asked him the significant question, "What do you do for fun?" It had been years since he had had any fun. On impulse, this child had thought it would be fun to smash the windshields.

The most frequent question I ask any client is, "What do you do for fun?" Most of the troubled youth respond, with depressed expressions, "Nothing." Fun can make a significant difference in the quality of living. Children do not know why they do the things they do—they react spontaneously. Much of the time they commit delinquent acts because they think it might be fun.

If there is anything we as parents must do, it is have fun with our children. They do not have to become giggly or silly, just happy.

Having fun does not come naturally. The art is learned, and most troubled youth have not had a parent, teacher, or minister to teach them. They think what they do is fun. It is no coincidence that they use the word "high." Many kids have said it is fun to get high, it is fun to be on drugs, fun to be stoned. They think it is better than sitting at home or

89

in school being bored. I do not believe the myth that most children get high because they are escaping something. I think most children are not escaping from something that is there; rather they are reaching for something that is not there.

God gives to every child "according to his ways, according to the fruit of his doings." As the child learns to experience good, fun activities, he is blessed.

> Blessed is the man who makes the Lord his trust. (Psalm 40:4, RSV)

As parents we trust the Lord to teach us to laugh with our children.

PTA mother. A mother raised her hand during a Parent Teacher Association meeting. She was disturbed because she could not make her child get out of bed in the morning, make his bed, eat his breakfast, or get to school on time. By the time she finished describing his behavior, she was in tears.

I asked how old he was.

"Seven," was her answer.

I asked if she could make him smile. I explained, "I guarantee you that if you do not make the child smile, it will be tough to make him do anything else."

If we do not teach our children love and faith, have fun with them, and give them something to smile about, chances increase that we will someday find them at juvenile court.

If we have a good relationship with our sixteen-year-old son, we say firmly, "Son, it is Saturday morning and time to clean out the garage." The usual responses are: "Why do I have to clean out the garage?"; "I always have to do every-thing"; and, "No one ever does anything but me."

The boy might then remember that he went fishing with his father the weekend before, and he will go spend ten minutes straightening the junk in the garage. But if we have a bad relationship we tell the boy to clean the garage and instead he will go to be with "those brats down the street."

Those brats usually are blamed for all of our child's problems; but he has a relationship with them, and he would rather take the risk of being with them, regardless of what he will have to face when he gets home.

Many youth can recall some good times in their lives when they had fun with grandparents. One youth told me the last time he was good for any period of time was when he stayed with his grandparents. He said it was fun listening to Grandpa tell the same story for the twentieth time. He giggled at what was left out or added.

The youth also laughed at Grandma's burned cookies. I am convinced that if we had more of Grandma's burned cookies, we would have less unruly children. Grandparents complain that they do not know what to say about drugs, alcohol, etc. But it is not what we say, it is what we do that makes the difference. Making cookies communicates love, fun, and acceptance. Grandparents' houses often are ha-vens, particularly for grandchildren on the run. Grandpar-ents sometimes feel out of the mainstream of childraising, when actually the effectual fervent prayers of righteous grandparents avail much.

HOPE

For I know that my Redeemer lives, and at last he will stand upon the earth. (Job 19:25, RSV)

91

Hope, the fourth guideline in the rearing of responsible children, is perhaps the most difficult. To be fulfilled, a child must feel that he is going to have a good life, that life is going to be worth living. If he feels that nothing is going to work out for him, he will have a miserable existence.

The theology of hope is a belief that God gives gifts to each one of us. We need to convey to our children that it is good to be alive, and that because Christ Jesus lives, they have the hope to face tomorrow. As parents we can instill in our children an awareness of the presence of Christ.

Krista's song. About 5:30 one morning the thunder was rolling and the lightning flashing, and I could hear our three-year-old, Krista, fussing. I waited for my wife to get up. Finally, there was that inevitable poke, and the words, "It's your turn."

Why is it always my turn? Just as I was about to open the door, I realized Krista was not frightened anymore. She was humming, and then she began to sing, "I can hear Him in the thunder, I can see Him in the lightning, I can feel Him in the rain. My Lord is with me all the time."

By the time our children go to school, they should be aware that Jesus Christ is with them all the time. They will need the hope and knowledge of his presence to face problems and temptation with their peers.

When I worked at the Kentucky State Reformatory, I sensed very quickly a lack of hope in the men. A man who is a "lifer," or even a man with a six-year sentence seldom feels that the next day will be better. It is very difficult to try to be a rehabilitated man if there is no hope that rehabilitation will make any difference.

A child should know every day that his Redeemer lives and that he is very near. Through his faith in Christ, in himself, and in others, the child can wake up in the morning with a hope of having a good day. He can end a day with the hope that the next day, the next week, and the rest of his life will be good!

Children feel better about themselves knowing that God is with them—not to judge, but to love. Once our daughter Trina listened silently as Mr. George Beverly Shea beautifully sang on a record, "God will take care of you." A few minutes later the three-year-old asked who God was. Joyfully I explained that he was Jesus' Father and our Heavenly Father. Trina asked if God would take care of her. I assured her he would. "Good," she exclaimed. "Then I don't have to go to day-care tomorrow."

4
HOW
TO AVOID
EMOTIONAL
TRAPS

The responsible child has learned to experience the giving and receiving of love. He develops faith in himself and in God. He has fun. He relaxes in a feeling of hope. These four qualities build success and produce happiness. A child suffers definite pain if he lacks any one of these characteristics.

This chapter deals with ways in which a child seeks to avoid this pain. A child's emotions and behavior (see chapter 5) are symptoms of how he feels about himself, his situation, and the world around him. This chapter presents difficulties as revealed through emotional symptoms.

These symptoms are the extremes, and certainly exaggerations of normal family problems. As we study these symptoms, we learn the traps to avoid and, to some extent, the treatment for such situations. Prevention is the best treatment.

THE FAILURE CHILD

> Then God said, "Let us make man in our image, after
> our likeness. . . . " (Genesis 1:26, RSV)

It takes a long, gradual process of failure for a child to
become failure-oriented; it takes an even longer time for a
failure-oriented child to become success-oriented. God has
created each child with great potential. Some children
must work harder than others, but each child has the
potential for some competence.

Fox. A child might follow the same pattern as in the classic
fable of the two foxes (as I have modified it). The fable
begins with a robust fox who had everything "together"
and was plainly successful. As he strutted through the
woods, a little bit hungry, he looked up and saw a bunch of
grapes which were bigger than the ordinary grapes. Immediately he was famished. He reached up and missed them.
He was not accustomed to missing anything.

He ran, leaped, and missed again—and again. As he considered what might be wrong, up walked a puny little fox.
Puny little fox looked up, saw those grapes, and seemingly
with no effort at all, brought down a nice bunch and began
eating them. Robust fox jumped the fourth time and
missed, noticing that Puny was watching. That humiliated
him, so with all the strength he could muster, he leaped
and missed a fifth time.

He asked Puny to share. Puny declared, "Get your own."

For a sixth and final time, Robust fox took a long run and
reached as high as he could, only to miss again. He sat
down and perhaps wondered why there were so many evil,
puny foxes in the world who would not share with him.
He wondered what was wrong with him that he could not

make it, wondered why God had not given him stronger legs.

Finally he said, "Oh, well, I wasn't really hungry. I really didn't want those grapes. Besides, they were probably sour." This attitude is commonly called "sour grapes," and often describes a failure-oriented child.

A failure-oriented child cannot face "high" expectations. The child, of course, is expected to continue to complete high school. But according to him, all the teachers hate him and single him out, all the other kids are picking on him, and besides, education is not important.

The failure-oriented child eventually leaves Akron in search of the ten-dollar-an-hour job in California. He finds life too difficult, and he settles for something less than he ever would have believed possible, because he cannot make the effort to become the successful person he should be. The child often says, "Forget it." Or, "Who cares?" Or simply, "It is not worth it." To him, it is not.

When a child feels he is a failure, we must work with him on very short-range goals. At the beginning of our counseling, these goals are usually easily achievable in a day so that the child can feel successful in accomplishing even the smallest tasks. This principle also works in the home. As the child experiences some success, he begins to realize the potential of his creation.

THE DEPRESSED CHILD

> He drew me up from the desolate pit, out of the miry bog, and set my feet upon a rock, making my steps secure. (Psalm 40:2, RSV)

Depression is a symptom of the inner heart. A child may find it easier to be depressed than to feel the pain of the lack of love, faith, fun, and hope in his life. However, a child does not often feel comfortable in sitting, withdrawing, and staring. Thus a depressed child sometimes seems more active than an equally depressed adult.

Popcorn man. One of my first depressed clients was a seventeen-year-old youth who had been depressed to some degree for over two years. His case study revealed that he had dropped out of high school, got a job, and married. When he was laid off from work, he went into a deep depression, feeling worthless. His wife whined many times a day, "Why don't you find a job?"

He talked to me about this for ten minutes, which is my limit before I begin feeling depressed myself.

I surprised him by saying, "I agree with you that you should feel depressed."

He quizzed, "You do?"

"Of course I do." Then I asked, "Tell me, why can't you cheer up?"

He answered, "Because I'm depressed."

I knew if we talked only about the depression, he would just get worse. So I changed the subject from emotions to behavior by asking him to describe a typical day.

He said, "For the last three months, all I have felt like doing is sleeping until noon, watching soap operas, and eating popcorn."

That would depress anyone. I wondered why, after three months, he wanted to change. He fidgeted in his chair and said, "To tell you the truth, my popcorn popper broke."

I encouraged him to become involved in a church where he and his wife could find caring people. There he learned that God loved him, that he was bought with a price—the blood of Christ. This gave him self-worth.

He joined the volunteer program at the juvenile court, and had fun with a troubled younger boy, which probably helped him more than the boy. His wife joined him in marriage counseling. She stopped whining, "Why don't you go out and find a job?"

One day he called and exclaimed, "My depression lifted and I found a job." He was lifted from the miry bog. Praise God.

HOSTILE CHILD

> But if any one strikes you on the right cheek, turn to him the other also. (Matthew 5:39, RSV)

Judge William P. Kannel of the Summit County Juvenile Court feels that we are living in an age when many people are hostile. People are angry at their neighbors; kids are angry at their parents; parents are angry at their kids; kids can't get along with teachers; and teachers are frustrated at kids. There is hostility everywhere. I am sure it is easier to feel hostile than to feel the pain of a lack of love, faith, fun, and hope. I'm sure many children are hostile simply because they do not know how to channel their energy into fun activities.

It is not a deliberate choice. Every child has energy, and he must do something with it. Unfortunately, too often it is easier to label a child as simply being hopelessly hostile than to go through the difficult healing process with him, developing the characteristics necessary to achieve peace.

Douglas' choices. During my initial session with him, Douglas, fifteen years old, grinned as he gestured in description of how he beat his younger brothers, set fires, pulled the heads from small animals, and drowned cats. His daydreams were of carefully planned violence. Even his parents—particularly his mother—were literally terrified of him. Doug's ambition in life was to be an undercover agent in many different foreign countries, so that he could legally "waste" people.

The child had been through several series of psychological and physiological examinations. He would not take any medication, as he did not want to stifle his "creativity." He steadfastly claimed to be "very religious."

After attending the first two months of weekly sessions, he became less aggressive as he achieved success in the school wrestling program. Doug achieved only partial success in the Boy Scout program because of so many conflicts with his peers and the leaders. Church youth activities for him were a total disaster.

After several months he tried unsuccessfully to run away. In his flight, he fell into a hole and injured his head on a rock. He interpreted this as a sign from God. A little while later he was admitted to a psychiatric unit after stabbing himself with a hunting knife during a history class. He was involved in two episodes while in the psychiatric unit. After fourteen trouble-free days he was released to his parents, a psychiatrist, and me. However, he never saw his psychiatrist, and he refused to take his medication, claiming that it reduced his athletic ability. I pointed out to him that he had three choices: (1) take his medication; (2) be institutionalized; (3) become so responsible that the first two were unnecessary.

He was furious at first. Soon he began to show quiet restraint, and became open about hurts and more realistic about changes. It had taken over a year and a half. Finally, with much pain he discussed his parents' poor marriage and his constant struggle to keep them together. Fortunately, he was able to pressure them into marriage counseling.

Life is not easy for Doug, but he is becoming responsible for his actions and accepting hurts in his life realistically rather than exhibiting inappropriate hostility. He is learning to approach life by challenging hurts with kindness rather than with increased hostility.

THE SUICIDAL CHILD

> Christ in you, the hope of glory. (Colossians 1:27, RSV)

Suicide is at least the second leading cause of death among young people, and one wonders whether it figures in some of the tragedies reported as accidents. Sometimes youth seek to use emotional symptoms as a way of running from pain. The ultimate end of running away is, of course, suicide. Even in these extreme cases, the theology of God's presence on earth and the theology of hope can bring healing.

Knit for life. Dealing with a suicidal teen is always a stressful here-and-now situation. I had been counseling for the Protestant Youth Counseling Service only a few months when a young woman client came to say, "Good-bye, and thanks for the four sessions." She was carrying an empty bottle as proof she would be dead in a few minutes.

103

I urged her to voluntarily have her stomach pumped. She said she would run if I called an ambulance. She only wanted to talk.

I quickly began telling her of the unsearchable riches of Christ, and that God loved her. But she would not listen to either a religious or a psychological approach.

Since she was an obese girl and I knew she enjoyed humor, I said, "I feel sorry for your pallbearers. They will all get hernias."

I got her attention!

"Besides," I continued, "all your chins are going to look funny while you lie in the casket." I suggested she reduce before suicide.

She began to think.

I asked her about her family.

"I hate 'em all," she snapped.

I told her I did not think it was fair not to express this to them.

I asked about her little boy.

She said she loved him very much.

I did not think it was fair for her to leave him, but she was sure he would be better off without her. I advised that she knit him a beautiful afghan to express her love.

It worked! She went to the hospital and had her stomach pumped.

There we made a simple plan. She was to complete the following: (1) Lose two pounds; (2) tell her mother she hated her; (3) recite her husband's faults to him; (4) knit the afghan for her son; (5) read the Gospel of John.

I told her I would pray that something would happen to change her life.

Releasing her bottled-up feelings to her husband brought so much satisfaction that she started to go see her mother to do the same. However, as she was running to her car, she slipped and fell on a patch of ice, breaking her arm.

She called me that night, furious. Remembering my closing statement during the counseling session, she was sure both God and I had tricked her, causing her to break her arm, which prevented her from knitting the afghan for her son.

After she had finished screaming, my response was, "Maybe all things do work together for good."

Eventually she completed the first plan and several others as well, and suicidal symptoms receded after her success.

THE PSYCHOSOMATIC CHILD

> The Lord Jesus Christ, who will change our lowly body to be like his glorious body, by the power which enables him even to subject all things to himself. (Philippians 3:20, 21, RSV)

The psychosomatic child is ill. At times children become ill because it is easier to be sick than to feel the pain of the reality of their situations.

Debbie's pain. Every time Debbie came for counseling she had a different complaint. I think she consulted the medical dictionary.

One day she complained, "My arm is just killing me."

"It can't be."

"Why not?" she retorted.

I reminded her that it was her arm that hurt the previous week.

"Oh, now it's my leg."

She came in with a terrible headache on one visit after we had established a level of trust. I told her it was all in her head.

One theory states that perhaps as many as 76 percent of hospitalized youth are without accurate diagnosis.

Debbie welcomed a stay in the hospital. The staff was attentive; people visited, sent flowers and cards, and said nice things. Even the preacher visited.

The child felt loved and important.

The average stay in some hospitals is eight days, but Debbie stayed ten. After eight days even the preacher was busy with someone else. The flowers faded and the cards fell from the wall. So Debbie went home where someone was glad to see her and showered her with attention—for a while.

When the attention faded, the child got sick again. She was feeling actual physical pain, but it is easier to cope with that than the pain of being ignored or frustrated.

Debbie would rather feel the pain of a bad leg than the pain of a bad life. But she needed to feel just as loved while she was well as while she was sick. She also needed help to accomplish something requiring greater skill than being sick. At least she needed to be encouraged to talk with confidence about something else. The only thing Debbie could discuss well was her operation, even over dinner.

Generally, the more active a child can be, the better, even if the activity must be gained very slowly through a gradual plan of achievements.

In this case, Debbie's body began to change because of changes inside her. The more times she experienced success, the less she needed to have a failing body. Specifically, Debbie discovered a talent for color coordination and design which eventually led her to study in the field of interior decorating.

THE PSYCHOTIC CHILD

> Who shall separate us from the love of Christ? Shall
> tribulation, or distress, or persecution, or famine, or
> nakedness, or peril, or sword? (Romans 8:35, RSV)

If a child were to live in an environment where he heard
only ridicule, hostility, and negative reactions, and if there
were little hope that life would be better, we could understand why he might act and speak in such a way as to be
diagnosed as psychotic. But even psychosis cannot separate
us from the love of Christ.

Friend George. Jerry was referred for counseling by a
teacher because he was almost totally withdrawn, except
when he talked to "George." No one in his class was named
George.

The teacher noticed Jerry gradually talking more and
more about and to George, and less and less to anyone else.
His parents never noticed.

"George is a good friend," said Jerry, who had no others.
One day he laughed loudly in class, saying that George
thought his art project was really good.

"George makes me laugh. We have fun. He really likes
me," the seventeen-year-old enthusiastically proclaimed.

During the second session, George joined us. Jerry spent
the entire session talking about and to George. He left
smiling. I cried.

It was easier for Jerry to talk to George than to face the
reality of his situation.

After working in three mental hospitals, and after being
in practice for ten years, I am convinced that many who
become psychotic choose to do so. Perhaps the choice is
not a conscious one; it is not that they get up in the

morning and say, "I am going to go nuts." It is simply easier to "talk to George" than to face reality. As I have counseled with many "pre-psychotic" youth, I have wondered why it has taken some of the kids so long to slip into this unreality.

> I consider that the sufferings of this present time are not worth comparing with the glory that is to be revealed to us. (Romans 8:18, RSV)

Mr. B. Psychotic patients have gifts to offer.

As a college psychology major, my first practice patient was Mr. "B."

I walked into a room with heavily screened windows and sat behind a desk. I was told my patient had a diagnosis of "paranoid schizophrenia," which meant to me that he was afraid of people.

I was afraid of him. I quickly reviewed all of the characteristics and treatment plans for paranoid schizophrenics, and quickly made notes. As he was escorted down the hall, somehow his five-foot-four frame seemed six foot ten.

He smiled and said, "How do you do?"

I was too frightened to say anything. He was fine. I was glad one of us was!

We looked at each other and then—I shall never forget—with a very kind expression on his face, he said with sympathy, "It's all right, I won't hurt you."

I breathed a too-loud sigh of relief.

He really looked concerned when he asked how I felt about being there.

"I'm a little nervous," I responded. I had planned to ask him that same question.

Softly, he asked, "Would you like to talk about it?" I did, and I was surprised to feel better.

"I believe Jesus Christ can help us," he testified, just as I had planned to testify.

I went back for fifteen weeks. I got much better.

He was a kind man who simply could not deal with stress in one particular area. He was fine as long as that area could be avoided.

During the weeks he discussed this area and his confidence grew. He got better because he knew he was giving something: He was helping me.

THE GRIEVING CHILD

> Peace I leave with you; my peace I give to you; not as the world gives do I give to you. Let not your hearts be troubled, neither let them be afraid. (John 14:27, RSV)

Bubble gum boy. Many children react aggressively to grief.

As the fourteen-year-old boy was aggressively escorted into my office by his grandfather, he gave me "the look" to let me know his disgust with the court and me. His grandfather whispered for him to dispose of his gum. The child sat with his arms tightly folded and his head down.

I smiled, told my name, and asked his. No answer.

As he frowned even more, he chewed his gum.

I asked if he enjoyed his gum.

No answer.

I asked if he could blow a bubble.

He saw his chance. He looked directly into my eyes, vigorously worked his gum, and stuck out his tongue through the gum.

I smiled.

He worked the gum again and slowly formed a small bubble.

I praised him.

He said he could do better, worked the gum faster, and blew a bigger bubble.

I praised him again.

He said he could do even better, and he did. The fourth bubble was as big as his face. It popped into his hair and over his right eye. I broke up.

He looked at me through the gum, and slowly, he too laughed.

Through his tears the grandfather shared that the child had not smiled since the death of his grandmother six months earlier. It took several sessions before the boy's heart was no longer as troubled.

> And I will pray the Father, and he shall give you another Comforter, that he may abide with you forever. (John 14:16, KJV)

Choices in grief. A child must learn to respond appropriately to grief.

For years Scott had not been getting along with his mother. In fact, they had argued that morning. It was not unusual when he was called to the principal's office, but this time was different—much different.

He was told that his mother was dead—murdered. The paper described the mother as the "victim," but Scott was also a victim. His incorrigibility festered into hostility and then exploded into rage.

He did not seem to have a conscience about delinquent and violent behavior. Drugs, alcohol, and sex became a way of continuing to live; but, in his words, "There is never a time when I don't remember."

Church and religion seemed meaningless to him. In shop class he made weapons. In other classes he daydreamed about how he would use the weapons. His only release was fighting, which became a contagious disease. Yet many times he was pleasant.

One evening a crisis occurred. He "booked" (ran). I found him—he wanted me to.

Suddenly he began to sob, pound his fists against the car dashboard, and yell as loudly as possible—but that was not enough. Later that evening he made plans for school and for better conduct. However, his resolve was short-lived. In a violent episode he smashed his hand through a window and required several stitches.

Soon thereafter, he swore he was going to kill his sister. I believed him and had him admitted to a psychiatric unit.

After eight days and many tests by skilled and competent professionals, the child was diagnosed as "emotionally unstable—character disorder." He refused medication.

I clarified for him his three choices: (1) Take the medication; (2) be institutionalized; (3) be responsible. He cried, but agreed to assume responsible behavior. He is also taking some medication.

He seems better and is calmer; but at this writing I am still very fearful for him and pray daily that God will protect him from himself, and that he will accept Christ, who alone can comfort him forever.

5

PROBLEM
BEHAVIORAL
SYMPTOMS

The "problem child" is most generally characterized as such because of "bad" behavior. Just as emotional symptoms are often indicative of feelings of lack of love, faith, fun, and hope, so are behavioral problems. A child's "bad" behavior is usually a symptom of his pain. It is easier to be "bad" than to feel pain.

In this chapter, as in chapter four, we are presenting extreme situations. The case studies illustrate guidelines for parents of normal children who sometimes have problems. The reader is advised to be aware of the circumstances which led to the problem behavior as a way of attempting to avoid such circumstances. It is easier to prevent problem behavior than to find ways to change it.

My first encounter with serious behavioral symptoms was when I was employed at the Kentucky State Reformatory in LaGrange, Kentucky. The institution had an average population of 1,812 men. I held positions of case worker, group counselor, Director of Admission and Orientation Unit, and Coordinator of Casework Services. Before starting a therapy group, I administered a personality inventory to men who were in group therapy, and to a control group that was not in therapy. Three months later I gave the same test to both groups. It was a traumatic experience for me as I scored those tests and discovered that the men involved in my group were somewhat more hostile, more deviant, and more violent than they had been when they were admitted. Then I scored the control group and discovered that the men were significantly more hostile, more violent, and more deviant. I began to wonder about the way we as society deal with criminals, particularly when considering the high rate of recidivism.

Recidivism was caused not so much by the inmate going out into a community where he was not loved or accepted, as by his inability to cope with all the hostility that built up during the months or even years he was in the institution.

One of my responsibilities was classification. A man aggressively entered my office with his rehearsed story. The men in the "fish tank"—Admission and Orientation Unit—practiced with each other answering questions that I might have asked. They had nothing else to do. This man said he wanted a prestigious job in the tag plant because, even though the pay was almost nothing, it would provide some money he could send home to his family.

He continued, with tears streaming down his cheeks, "I am the only one that my children have now. They don't have a mother; I am in here, and I must support them. So you just must give me that tag plant job."

It was sad. Then I looked at his sentence in order to determine if custody could be granted. He was serving a life sentence on a charge of murder. He was a widower because he had killed his wife. He had not learned to assume responsibility for his behavior.

SONNY: OUR FOSTER CHILD

My first real experience with a youth with serious behavior problems was quite personal. Not long after I became associated with the Juvenile Court Center, Ann and I took responsibility for a sixteen-year-old boy, whom we called "Sonny."

Sonny had been in many different placements before he came to live with us. We loved Sonny and wanted the best for him, but I guess we did not realize how hard it would be to break through his shell of hostility.

We gave him his own room and bathroom. We put our stereo in his room. I found him a job at a local car wash. Ann enrolled him in a night school where he could study toward his GED—General Education Diploma.

We tried to do everything we knew that was best for Sonny. But the toughest thing was trying to get him out of bed in the morning. I pounded on the door, then went and told Sonny it was time to get up. I kept going back again and again.

How frustrating it became day after day! As I read a chapter in a book entitled *Love Your Child,* I looked for advice as to how to get Sonny out of bed in the morning.

I soon learned he was smoking pot all night on our back porch. He thought anyone who worked was a fool. Sonny had his own ideas about living and was going to do things his way, regardless of our pleadings.

He left his pills lying around the house where our two-year-old, Laura, could easily get them.

He joined the service and went AWOL. He had fallen into a frequent pattern: When in trouble, run. He wrote for money for quite some time, and we sent it.

Sonny taught us many things, especially that it is never enough only to love, however deeply. We must apply the

117

love daily with practical wisdom. Sonny taught us that we must first learn the values the child holds, before we can expect to make decisions which are "best for him."

We discovered later that many of the decisions we had made were meaningless. We needed first to discover how to get the kid out of bed in the morning!

THE UNRULY CHILD

An unruly child, by definition, commits a crime which is peculiar only to a child. A delinquent child commits an offense which is also unlawful for an adult. But to many parents an unruly child is loosely defined as any child having "bad" behavior.

> If any of you lacks wisdom, let him ask God, who gives to all men generously and without reproaching, and it will be given him. (James 1:5, RSV)

Truancy is the most frequent unruly behavior reported to us. Many children do not go to school because they do not like it: "It's no fun"; "The teachers are mean"; and, "None of the other kids like me." Sometimes a child will admit that it is just too hard, as was discussed in the section, "The Failure Child."

Tracy's ultimate responsibility. Tracy had missed school an average of two days a week over a three month period. The question was asked, "Who has the ultimate authority in this case?" The teacher discussed class participation expectations with Tracy. The unit principal demanded attendance.

Finally the child and family were referred to the board of education, pupil personnel department.

118

Threats were made. Alternative schools were presented without satisfaction. This irresponsible child had irresponsible parents.

Further absences led to a referral to juvenile court. Threats were made by court personnel. The child was counseled and released.

The responsibility had to be Tracy's. Her parents did not have the proper control over this fifteen-year-old, and no one was going to drag her to school every day. Even if that were possible, no one could make her learn. Her choice was to take care of herself.

The truant child needs much stroking for the successful completion of many short-term, easily obtainable, realistic goals.

On Tracy's first visit, she read with difficulty the plaque on my wall: "If any of you falls short in wisdom, ask God for it and it shall be yours." She responded, "Nuh-uh." I responded, "Uh-uh." She, "Nuh-uh," I, "Uh-uh."

I asked her to try praying at night that God would help her get out of bed the next morning. I asked her to pray this each evening and each morning. She did, and she made it to school four out of five days.

When she came back to my office three weeks later, she read the plaque again and responded, "Uh-uh."

> Study to shew thyself approved unto God, a workman that needeth not to be ashamed, rightly dividing the word of truth. (2 Timothy 2:15, KJV)

Eraser-throwing kid. Many youth with school problems have home problems as well.

A little five-year-old boy was referred to me because he

had the habit of hitting his kindergarten teacher in the back of the head with erasers. I do not know where he got all the erasers.

Traditional counseling had proved unsuccessful.

I have toys in my counseling office, and we played on the floor with little cars. We had a great deal of fun; he was a nice little kid. But when his mother heard what we were doing, she said, "I pay him to do that?"

The mother and teacher kept asking the child why he threw the erasers. I knew that asking "why" was not helpful. When interrogated, the child became defensive and immediately distant. Usually he responded, "I don't know," because, of course, he did not know.

Most youth do not know why they do what they do; they just do it, spontaneously.

I asked him a behavioral question instead: "What happens when you throw the erasers?"

With a big smile he said, "The teacher calls me by name."

I asked if she always did that.

"No, sometimes her face gets red and she mumbles something."

I believed him. He loved to hear his name. It was all he had that was only his.

When we praise our children, we should use their names. When we scold, it is better not to use their names.

I made a contract with this child and his teacher. The child was to spend five minutes two mornings a week dusting erasers. I thought that was appropriate. During the time before class, the teacher was to talk to him about how important his task was, and to call him by name.

Soon he was not throwing erasers anymore. I also noticed during a session of playing cars that the child was upset because he had heard his parents screaming at each other in the waiting room.

Eventually they came to me for marriage counseling. The child and the parents even began having family devotions. The parents started getting along better. And guess who stopped throwing erasers?

> And he arose and came to his father. But while he was yet at a distance, his father saw him and had compassion, and ran and embraced him and kissed him. (Luke 15:20, RSV)

It would be impossible to estimate the number of runaways in this country each year.

Why do some kids have so much pain that they run from their parents to almost anything or anyone else? Jesus described a runaway boy in the parable of the Prodigal Son.

The prodigal. At six o'clock in the morning, the phone rang. Bryan's mother was extremely upset. She had just discovered that her son had not slept in his bed that night. She was sure he had run away and would be killed, "He's so small for sixteen."

She had good reason to be panic-stricken after the years of problems with Bryan—particularly with drugs.

As she talked she expressed frustration, worry, hurt, anger, and then hopelessness. I offered the usual advice about calling the police and filing a missing persons report. Then I testified, "I don't know whether you are a Methodist, a Baptist, Orthodox, or what you are, but right now you need God."

I concluded, "I want you to pray for help now for both

you and Bryan. Also pray for strength for just the right moment to act." She asked when the moment would come. I told her she would know.

At two o'clock the next afternoon I was traveling down the expressway. By divine guidance, I'm sure, I spotted Bryan hitchhiking. I drove up a little ahead of the young man and unlocked my car doors. Without a glance, the kid ran to me and jumped into the car. I locked the doors, stepped on the gas, looked over, and smiled, "Hi, Bryan!"

He said, "You're going to lock me up, aren't you?"

I asked him how he was doing. He threw his shoulders back. Nothing was going to hurt this kid—he had it all together. Everyone else was wrong.

"I'm doing great, I've never done better," he said. Then, looking at me, he continued, "In fact, I'm doing better than you are."

I could tell it was going to be difficult. I asked him if he had had any lunch.

He retorted, "You know, I hate you."

We weren't exactly clicking. So I said, "Did you happen to have any breakfast this morning?"

He thought for a moment, threw his shoulders back again, sat up as high as he could, and offered, "You are the biggest jerk I have ever met."

I asked about dinner the night before. He thought for another moment and blurted out, "You know, I don't like God either." Of course he knew that would get to any preacher.

Knowing I had to praise him for something, anything, I said, "I'm glad you believe in God enough not to like him."

One of us laughed and I drove on, nearing a McDonald's. I had had a speaking engagement that afternoon, and had

had bland chicken over biscuits. I was still hungry, so I asked the boy if he wanted anything too.

He reminded me he was doing great and did not need me, my food, or my God; but he thought he could force himself to eat something.

I knew I could tell more about the child by the way he ate than by anything he said. He asked if we could go inside to eat, but I do not like for a child to eat and run.

He leaned his lanky body across me, held onto the steering wheel, and tried to whisper his order into the drive-up box. He whispered a long time. The clerk did not repeat the order. She only said, "OK, whatever."

I knew then I was in trouble. I could not believe it when the lady handed me all those white bags. From the price, I thought I was buying stock. The child almost inhaled two Big Macs!

As we pulled back into the parking lot, he asked, "Well, are you going to lock me up or not?" He acted as if he were the authority.

I responded, "If I don't lock you up, where would you go?"

"Home, I want to go home; please take me home." I reminded him that he had told his mother he hated her, was going to run away forever, never wanted to see her again—and a few other things. He said he did not mean the things he had said. He, too, was angry and frustrated.

Then I dug deeper, "Tell me specifically what you would do if I let you go home." I could tell he was thinking because he was eating one French fry at a time from his order of large fries. He had stuffed the whole small fry order into his mouth at once.

He said, "Chaplain, preacher, if you let me go home, I will go to church every Sunday, I will even read my Bible, and I will even pray." He added he was praying even then, "God, make him let me go home."

I praised him and asked what he wanted God to do with him that day.

He was thinking; he was using a straw in his chocolate shake. That's significant, because he had gulped down his strawberry shake, and had spilled ice from his cola all over himself.

"Well, if you let me go home, I will go to school."

That is sure to hook any court worker. I told him I was glad, but that was tomorrow. I asked him what he would do today.

I could tell he was still thinking; he was just nibbling on his cherry pie. He had broken the apple pie into two pieces and stuffed them both into his mouth.

He grinned fiendishly, "I'll clean my room."

A sure response to hook any parent. I told him that was great, but he had to do more.

"Do more than clean my room?"

I nodded.

"But, preacher, you haven't seen my room!"

I wanted more.

He began thinking again; he was using the spoon to eat his hot fudge sundae. That, too was significant; he had eaten the caramel one with his fingers.

Then he told me he would clean up his whole house— sure to impress any father.

I asked him how long he would spend on it. "The rest of my life."

Since I thought that was a little long, I asked him to explain specifically what he would do that day.

He described how he would clean his room, vacuum the living room if he could get the vacuum sweeper going, and dust if he could find the rag.

124

I asked him if he saw any value in the commitments he had made.

He elaborated well upon the values of each and was really thinking. I could tell, again, because he was slowly chewing on his cookies. Then, as if he had been eternally enlightened, he smiled for the first time and proclaimed, "If you let me go home, I will even clean the bathroom."

I was hooked. If a sixteen-year-old boy promises to clean the bathroom, you know you have him.

I had been to his home before, yet this boy really seemed surprised when we pulled up in front of his house. I saw the silhouette of his mother in the window. I expected him to get out and run into the house, but he just sat there.

Finally he softly called me by my name. We had progressed now; it is amazing the things that can happen after Big Macs!

"Byron, you won't believe this, but I'm scared."

He was somewhat embarrassed as he requested, "Byron, would you go in with me? Would you stay with me?"

Cautiously I asked, "How long?"

"About three months."

I told him that was a little long. But I encouraged, "You know, there is someone who will stay with you today, tomorrow, and through three months."

Broadly he smiled; then he squared his shoulders, frowned, and said, "You're talking about God again."

"Yea, God!" I said, with thumbs up.

He said, "What do I have to do, pray?"

I suggested we pray together.

He gave the typical sixteen-year-old response of, "You pray first." So I bowed my head, praying, "God, please help Bryan right now; he needs it." Then he bowed his head and prayed, "Yes, God, I sure do." Short prayers are best in crisis.

We got out of the car and walked into the house. I remembered this from the fifteenth chapter of Luke: "And he arose and came to his father. But while he was yet a great way off, his father saw him and had compassion, and ran and embraced him and kissed him."

The mother saw her son and opened the door. She looked at me and said, "This must be that moment I was supposed to pray for."

I answered, "Yes, this is it." She never said a word to him, she just put her arms around the boy. He stood up straight, threw his arms out, clenched his fists, tightly closed his eyes, and gritted his teeth. Kindness, forgiveness—nothing was going to get to him.

His mother's mouth was moving. She was praying. Her eyes were tearing up.

I saw a miracle unfold. Slowly, the boy unclenched his fists; very slowly he hugged his mother. Her tears mixed with his and he said in a kind of desperation, "Oh, Mommy, if you let me stay home, I will even clean the bathroom." And he did.

The boy went to school the next day, and finished the year. He and his mother learned to go to church together, to pray together, to bowl together, and to eat Big Macs together.

Ours is a society in which pain causes people to try to escape. Some children find that running away is the way to escape all the pressures of home. The prodigal son's father could have said, "Listen, kid, as long as you live in my house, you are going to do as I say." Or he could have told him not to talk back and to cut out any sinful living. Such demands, of course, would not make sense without a relationship.

Some people wonder why the father let the boy go. These people must have never experienced the pain of such a child.

The prodigal son's father let him go in the first place. Not only did the kid run, he ran with his father's blessings and his father's money. As a matter of fact, we could even interpret this that the father not only let him go, but paid him to go.

The father had done perhaps everything he could to be good to the son, until he reached his limit, and with frustration said, "OK, then, go."

There are some children who must learn from their own bad experiences, and find that the grass is not greener over on the other side. Many children must learn that everyone will not accept them, and take them into their homes, and feed them for years as their parents do.

The most significant fact in the story of the prodigal son is that eventually the child felt the pain of what he was doing to himself. He broke under the struggles of life, and finally, when he got to the very bottom of his existence, the Bible says that he "came to himself."

Sometimes the only thing we can do for our child is to be with him until he reaches that point. How painful and frustrating. Probably the hardest thing we may ever have to do is wait until our child, whom we love very much, comes to himself.

The prodigal son decided that he had sinned. He finally decided he wanted to ask his father for forgiveness.

The father was not a distant one, but a father who was still waiting, still accepting—and who must have looked down the road thousands of times, until he saw someone approaching who might be his son.

We can only imagine the joy when the father recognized the distant figure to be his son. He did not wait for the son to come back and apologize. Pride was not the issue with the father.

Pride gets in the way of too many parents who want their child to repent for hurting them, and to give in first.

The father of the prodigal made the first move in running out to his son. When he saw him, he had compassion.

The father said nothing. He just ran out, embraced his son, and kissed him. The son was the first to speak, asking for forgiveness. That father did not respond by telling him how much trouble he had caused, or taking an opportunity to preach his favorite sermon. No, instead the father decided to throw a party.

Some might say the father was rewarding the "little brat." Parents so often want their runaway child locked up. But many runaways who are locked up only run farther the next time.

The father gave his son a robe, a ring, and shoes. All he asked was that his son be his son.

There is a happy ending to this story: "And they all began to be merry." It is a result everyone wants.

In the meantime, waiting is tough. Watching a child go through pain until he comes to himself and his God takes real strength. But there is hope in the parable of the prodigal son.

As we consider the runaway child, it is important also to realize the large number of parents who want to run away. One mother said that it was not fair; her child got away with bad behavior and he also "got to run away." She did not understand, however, the fear within a runaway child.

Parents who do run must live with the resultant guilt. Alternatives to running away are much more acceptable.

Often parents of runaways need the same feelings of affirmation as the children. Fighting this difficult problem requires listening and healing on both sides.

> "Well done, good and faithful servant; you have been faithful over a little, I will set you over much; enter into the joy of your master." (Matthew 25:23, RSV)

Many referrals to the court for curfew violations are the result of the police suspecting the child of a more serious charge. Nevertheless, curfew is a problem in a number of homes.

Some guidelines are: First, the curfew should be realistic, depending upon the area where the child lives. Second, curfew should depend upon the maturity of the child. Some youth are able to handle more responsibility than others.

Each community has its own curfew laws. Of course, youth may stay out later if they are with an adult, attending special functions, and or if adequate transportation arrangements have been made. Curfew should be earned. A child who is responsible over his homework and chores may receive consideration for a later curfew.

Curfew dispute. I often deal with differences of opinion on curfew.

The parents in one case were very possessive of their seventeen-year-old daughter. They had their own problems and did not want to let go. They set the curfew at 7:00 P.M. every evening.

The child ran away, of course; she wanted a curfew of 2:00 A.M. A difference of opinion led to a lack of trust, and much rebellion.

The girl finally agreed that things had to be better and said she was willing to work at it. The parents also agreed, but were reluctant to change. Nevertheless, the curfew was set at 7:30 P.M. for two weeks.

The girl did well. For the next two weeks, her curfew was 7:45. The girl wanted to stay out longer, but she was building trust. At least the tremendous tension in the home was reduced.

Fifteen minutes were added to her time every two weeks, until a final curfew was set at 9:30 during school nights and 10:30 on weekends. Later curfew permission was given under special conditions.

All seemed fine until one evening when the daughter was fifteen minutes late. The parents were furious. No explanation was acceptable to them. The 9:30 curfew was set back fifteen minutes to 9:15 for the next two weeks. As she became responsible for getting home by 9:15, she was given the "greater talent" of staying out until 9:30. Such it was in Jesus' parable of the talents. When someone makes good with what he is given, he is rightly given more.

Privileges are much like curfew. Trust is given as responsibility is shown. We must be careful as parents, however, that we are not withholding privileges because of our need to keep our child dependent upon us. But we also need to permit our child to remain a child regardless of social or peer pressure.

For instance, parents should be informed whether there is going to be an adult at a party. We should ask whether alcohol and drugs are likely to be present. But the basic responsibility for privileges does not lie with the parents; it rests with the child.

When a child asks to go to a party, we should not immediately respond "No!" We should ask about the details: "What are you going to do if someone offers you pot?"

"What are you going to do if someone rolls in a keg?" "What will you say when you notice everyone is leaving the room, and your date is asking if you want to check out the laundry room?"

We prepare our child all of his life for that particular moment, and then we pray constantly that God's overshadowing grace will abide with him that night, and forevermore. Prayerfully, our relationship will carry us and the child through the trusting process.

We need to remind the child of the spiritual values that have been a part of his home life. Then we consider realistically the request. There are times when we must answer an unashamed "No."

It is difficult at times to give responsibility to our children. I believe that by the time a child is thirteen he has had enough gradual training that he should bear the total responsibility for his own room. My practical theology is: It takes strength to say, "OK, it's your room," close the door, walk down the hall, and pray as you go. It is important to give a child the opportunity to find his own level of responsibility. How can we expect a child of eighteen to take full responsibility for his own life, if at age fifteen he cannot even begin to care for his own property?

If you are firm with a thirteen-year-old and do not waver, that child will learn from his success or failure. If he fails to clean his room, he won't be able to ignore the result, especially when he finds creatures in his closet! The same is true of clothing. If the child does not put his dirty clothes in the designated place at the proper time, they will not be washed. After a while he will notice, and other kids will notice, too. Naturally the mother will become embarrassed. But better the child be dirty at thirteen than delinquent at sixteen.

THE DELINQUENT CHILD

Most juvenile crime is situational. The circumstances of a child's life, coupled with a lack of coping strength, can propel the child into what seems an avalanche of poor choices. As we seek to reach the delinquent child, we try new ways of helping him to become responsible and accountable. Greater attention is being given to the chronic delinquent child, which amounts to less than 3 percent of the total number of youth referred to the juvenile court system.

> Be merciful to me, O God, be merciful to me, for in thee my soul takes refuge; in the shadow of thy wings I will take refuge, till the storms of destruction pass by. (Psalm 57:1, RSV)

Shotgun break. By number of court referrals, Jack was considered to be a delinquent child. His mother was panic-stricken one Saturday morning when she called. Her son had been pointing a shotgun at his older brother for more than an hour. The door to the bedroom was locked. Sixteen-year-old Jack kept yelling, "I'm going to kill him!" The older brother had "borrowed" his new designer jeans, which to him was a matter of life and death.

The police came to the home but were helpless. I had seen the youth only a few times. He finally agreed to talk with me, holding the gun in one hand and the phone receiver in the other. He shouted into the phone that he was going to kill his brother, and there wasn't anything I could do about it. At least he was talking with me.

I just asked him how he was doing. He recounted several tough situations and ended up by saying, "And now I am in this mess and there is no way of getting out of it." We both

132

knew the police were on the phone extension. I told him I thought there was a way out. I asked the boy what he had had for breakfast. He paused, and then described the orange juice, eggs, toast, and milk.

At that point, I heard the officer say, "He's talking about breakfast! Who did you say he is?" I asked the boy if he had had a large glass of juice, and he had. I asked if he had had a large glass of milk; he had.

Then I said, "You know, a crisis like this can bring people together. I consider you to be my friend. So, friend, I want to ask you a personal question."

He agreed.

I asked, "Have you gone to the bathroom since you drank the large glasses of milk and juice?"

He had not, and he had eaten two and a half hours earlier.

I asked if he had considered going to the bathroom.

Sarcastically, he said he had been considering it a lot since we had been talking about it.

I asked him if he really wanted to kill his brother.

He did not.

He agreed to go to the bathroom—which, of course, would require that he put down the gun. He also agreed to go with the police to juvenile court and meet me there. Before he hung up the boy thanked me.

Jack had let his life get out of control, and he did not know how to straighten it out gracefully. Many youth need a way out of their delinquent behavior and into responsible behavior. I worked with this boy to help him control his anger through alternative behavior. God was merciful; the boy found refuge and the storm of destruction passed him by.

THE PREGNANT CHILD

> I appeal to you therefore, brethren, by the mercies of God, to present your bodies as a living sacrifice, holy and acceptable to God, which is your spiritual worship. (Romans 12:1, RSV)

In order for a boy under eighteen and a girl under sixteen to be married in Summit County, they must have the consent of their parents, counseling by a professional, and the consent of the juvenile court. In my role as chaplain, I talk with many of the youth who wish to be married. Parental approval is not enough; the juvenile court must also approve. Four conditions are necessary: (1) financial stability; (2) housing; (3) parental approval; and (4) emotional stability. Children who marry because of pregnancy need much strength, guidance, and grace.

"In love" couple. The couple arrived over half an hour late to the appointment. I quickly noticed they both sat in the same small chair. They rather abruptly and naively told me they just wanted me to sign. I asked why they wanted to get married. They told me repeatedly how much they loved each other, and began to be rather free with their hands. I guess I was supposed to be impressed.

They were both sixteen; both had quit school. Neither was working, and the boy did not intend to work. He thought they could move in with her mother. Under the circumstances, I informed them that the court would not approve. He stood up and said, "Well, we have to get married. She's pregnant."

I told them that I thought the pregnancy indicated further irresponsibility, and that they could return when the young man had found a responsible job and demonstrated ability to be a husband and father.

The boy pointed his finger at me and loudly proclaimed, "I'm going to kill you!"

I then invited them to leave. They went beyond county limits, ignored the issues, and were married.

About eight months later, on a hot, late August morning, I was surprised to see them back. I could immediately tell something was different. They sat in separate chairs on opposite sides of the room. She began by saying what a "lazy bum" he was, and that all he did was drink and complain. He said she was a nag, a horrible housekeeper, and would not have sex. I asked about the baby. The couple had kept the baby for only two weeks, then they sent her to her grandmother. The baby cried too much.

In answering a question calling for specifics, the couple related that they had never decided who should take out the trash, so for months the trash had been thrown into a corner of their one-room apartment. This problem had brought them to me. August was very hot, and the trash smell had become unbearable.

I could not help but ask them about their previous declaration of all the love they had for each other. I could tell the boy had gained some wisdom during the previous eight months when he observed, "Love does not take out the trash." Like so many who marry so young, this couple divorced early.

Premarital pregnancies happen. Church youth directors, pastors, and Christian parents are shocked, disappointed, and sometimes shattered when one of their youth becomes pregnant. However, such situations are occurring with increased frequency. How often it seems that even the "good kids" are becoming pregnant. This seems to be of even more concern than the sexual activity of delinquent kids in detention. Many of the delinquent youth make a responsible decision concerning an irresponsible act, and choose "protection." Too many church youth naively follow the passion of the moment. How often I have heard, "We only did it once."

It is true that Jesus Christ gives strength to youth in such a way that they can abstain from intercourse. God gives us the strength to make a responsible decision. However, this theology must be communicated on a practical basis. It is not enough just to tell kids not to "do it," or for the youth to say to themselves or each other, "I know when to quit." The passion of the moment is greater than the theory of the week. The child must decide what value he or she places upon his or her body and upon virginity. A lot depends on the child's self-image in the first place. This helps determine how he will choose.

The child must learn how far is far enough long before a heavy sexual temptation occurs. Marriage is ordained by God, and the first act of intercourse is one of the finest of his gifts to the two who are joining their lives together. A youth must decide if the moment is to occur in the back seat of a car, during a hurried moment before anyone interrupts; whether it is to be done with some stranger, or if it is the fulfillment of God's purpose for marriage.

Sex is a beautiful experience when enjoyed without the pain of guilt. Good theology and a good self-image are successfully combined when a child realizes his or her body is a "temple." "What? know ye not that your body is the temple of the Holy Ghost which is in you, which ye have of God, and ye are not your own? For ye are bought with a price; therefore glorify God in your body, and in your spirit, which are God's" (1 Corinthians 6:19, 20, KJV).

The Bible well establishes that the appropriate place for sexual intercourse is within the covenant of the marriage relationship. "But because of the temptation to immorality, each man should have his own wife and each woman her own husband. The husband should give to his wife her conjugal rights, and likewise the wife to her husband" (1 Corinthians 7:2, 3, RSV).

There are four purposes for sexual intercourse within the marriage covenant. First, the sexual relationship consummates the union of "one flesh." "Have you not read that he who made them from the beginning made them male and female, and said, 'For this reason a man shall leave his father and mother and be joined to his wife, and the two shall become one flesh'? So they are no longer two but one flesh" (Matthew 19:4-6, RSV).

Second, sexual intercourse provides mutual pleasure for husband and wife. " . . . Rejoice in the wife of your youth, a lovely hind, a graceful doe. Let her affection fill you at all times with delight, be infatuated always with her love" (Proverbs 5:18, 19, RSV).

Third, sexual intercourse provides a profound, meaningful communication as a husband and wife experience each other in a mutual expression of love and intimacy. Scripture uses the word "know" as an indication of profound intimacy and communication between a man and his wife. "Now Adam knew Eve his wife, and she conceived and bore Cain, saying, 'I have gotten a man with the help of the Lord'" (Genesis 4:1, RSV).

Fourth, sexual intercourse is for the procreation of children. "And God blessed them, and God said to them, 'Be fruitful and multiply, and fill the earth and subdue it; and have dominion over the fish of the sea and over the birds of the air and over every living thing that moves upon the earth'" (Genesis 1:28, RSV).

> Do not be conformed to this world but be transformed by the renewal of your mind, that you may prove what is the will of God, what is good and acceptable and perfect. (Romans 12:2, RSV)

Abortion is not just a means of birth control. Julie's case story is an illustration of the pain that can result when it is treated as such.

Julie's abortion. Even after six months, two weeks, and three days of silence, the very religious mother still hurried to the phone, hoping against hope for the sound of her daughter, Julie's, voice.

Her heart pounded as she heard the soft question, "Mom, are you there?"

She was there then, but knew she had not been before. She choked up as she uttered an even softer, "Yes."

The daughter quickly and forcefully requested the mother to meet her at 9:00 the next morning at an abortion clinic. Smitten with inner pain, all the mother could manage was a faint, "Yes."

Of course she could not sleep. The mother had rehearsed her words and changed them over and over, but when she saw her daughter, no words came. How thin, frail, and hardened she looked, and so much older than fifteen. When eye contact was made, the mother was pierced with the sight of the girl's swollen, sunken, expressionless eyes. The excitement was gone, as was that boy who had always been around. Where was he now as she suffered through an abortion?

Mother and daughter embraced. No words spoken; only tears shed.

The short distance home seemed endless as the mother pointed out meaningless changes in the neighborhood.

The first day afterward Julie slept for hours—but at least she was home. Her mother had chicken soup ready for her when she finally awoke. There was so much more she wanted to give her. As the last bit of soup was being finished, hundreds of questions filled the mother's mind. These were bluntly pushed away by the anger, which had been held back for weeks—maybe months, maybe years.

The mother caught hold of herself. She prayed silently, intently. All she could do was crush crackers into smaller and smaller crumbs.

The daughter finally commented upon the condition of her room. Her mother wanted to remind her that it had looked that way for years, but instead suggested maybe they could spend some time fixing it up together.

Surprisingly, the tension was somewhat lessened as they pushed the trash around. The daughter found fragments of an old checkers game and suggested they play. They scrounged for almost anything to complete the set. The mother hoped the daughter would not notice her hands shaking.

The daughter had almost won the game when the phone rang. Her mother felt relieved that she did not have to race to the phone anymore. Her anger was barely in control when she heard the too-familiar voice. He asked for the daughter. The mother had to make a most important decision. She responded, "Just a moment, please." She was biting her lip as she walked from the kitchen.

She could not stand to hear her again-precious daughter talk to the boy whom she had denounced for months. She heard her daughter, however, quite emphatically say, "No!"

The mother paused at the door. The daughter continued, "I'm not coming back, at least not now. I'm having too much fun with my mother."

This mother regained her daughter. The time to preach, moralize, express rage, punish, and get even was over—if there ever was time for those reactions at all. The mother needed to learn not to throw the first stone.

It is not enough to say, "Wait until marriage," when many children are reaching puberty at age twelve, and many are not marrying until their middle or late twenties. What are the youth supposed to do for ten years?

A father told me recently that his son would not be involved in an unwanted pregnancy if he and his girl friend of five years had played Monopoly like he told them to do. It takes more than Monopoly as a second choice. Yet the idea is sound. Young people do need to find alternative activities. I often ask kids what they can do other than have sex. It takes a lot of creativity and imagination to find alternatives.

Youth today basically do not know how to have fun. Recently our high school administration asked me to speak to six classes of about seventy-five students each. The task: "Just tell them not to have sex." Good luck. The students and I talked together about personal worth and what they did for fun. Of course, they mentioned peer pressure to conform.

Trying to keep kids from having sex by laying on a guilt trip is becoming less and less effective. Certainly some kids have sex because they feel it is the only thing they can do well; it is the only fun they have. Such a child will not respond to the guilt approach.

As Christian parents we must be careful to avoid the trite reasons for not having sex. Some of the reasons adults used to give are nonsense to this generation. For years boys have been told not to use a girl as a "play thing" because it is not fair to the girl. Now girls are becoming more open about their own sexual feelings and some girls are even the sexual aggressors. Therefore, boys may feel sex is "OK" because the girls are using them as "play things" as well. Therefore, they say the act is not selfish; rather they are treating each other as persons.

Youth are told to wait until marriage before having sex, because this is God's plan for our greatest happiness; sex belongs within the context of marriage. One youth worker put it this way: "Premarital sex is like settling for a VW now when you can have a Cadillac later." The problem with this generation is that it would gladly accept a VW now, and any day of the week, instead of waiting five years for a Cadillac.

Fear alone does not work. This is not a generation which can easily be scared. Few youth believe they will become pregnant, let alone contract VD.

We must teach them that sex is God's good gift which he ordained for the enrichment and fulfillment of our lives. The sexual relationship was designed in creation! " . . . So God created man in his own image, in the image of God he created him; male and female he created them" (Genesis 1:27, RSV). God affirmed his creation to be good. "And God saw everything that he had made, and behold, it was very good" (Genesis 1:31, RSV).

Just as we cannot understand all of the reasoning of evil in the world, we cannot understand all about good either. Good sex is designed for the commitment of marriage, as an act of love.

> For this child I prayed; and the Lord has granted me my petition which I made to him. (1 Samuel 1:27, RSV)

"I love you, Baby." Giving a child up for adoption is one possibility for the pregnant child. Mary's case story reveals the pain of this alternative—but also the love.

As I hurried through a mall doing Christmas shopping, I was stopped by a nineteen-year-old girl whom I had known for several years. Small talk was brief. Then, cautiously and ashamedly, Mary related that she was pregnant. Quickly she told me she wanted more for her child than she had had herself. She asked me if I knew of any "good people" who would like to adopt her baby. I sensed how difficult it was for her even to ask the question. She talked emotionally of her love for her baby—a love so great she knew she had to give the baby up.

My wife Ann and I had friends who were childless. The couple had spent years and hundreds of dollars trying to have a child, and their frustration was intense. They had been on several agency lists for years. Nothing seemed to give them any hope at all, and the years were passing them by so quickly.

I noticed my hand shaking as I made the phone call of a lifetime and suggested to the woman, Jane, that the four of us get together soon—that night.

Later she recalled she thought the request was a little strange, but she also knew me. Bob even canceled a flying lesson. They both thought I was on another one of my campaigns and wanted their help.

When they arrived, the small talk seemed forced. Ann and I were definitely uptight. I noticed again how lovingly they related to our children. Their love and attention relaxed me and gave me the courage to risk what was ahead.

Ann's always-good coffee seemed tasteless. After the children left the room, I asked about their future plans, and the usual activities were discussed rather passively. When we asked about baby prospects, Bob told of yet another out-of-state clinic, and Jane told of yet another waiting list. Their monotone voices and forced half-smiles made me shake as I held my coffee cup.

To change the subject, and out of interest, Bob asked if there was anything new with my work. I told them that there was something completely new happening; and then as I cleared my dry throat, I suggested that there was a possibility they could help me. They both laughed and said they could tell I was up to something, but said, of course, they would be willing to help in any way they could.

I told them the "adventure" I had in mind required a great risk and the reward was remote. Not knowing what I meant, and not realizing that their entire lives were about to be changed, they agreed that they were "up to anything."

All I said was, "There is a girl." Jane buried her head in her hands before she fell backward on the couch. Words are completely useless in describing the emotional impact of the next few minutes. At times like that there never are enough tissues around.

Time was short. We began having long discussions with the girl. She was strong and sensitive—and logical. She was also immature, but she knew it. She knew she needed help a lot. A lawyer was retained for her; prenatal care began. Then she needed a different place to live. The "adoptive parents," as they proudly began to call themselves, also secured a lawyer. The situation became further complicated because the couple lived out of the county. The eager—to put it mildly—couple also feared the girl might change her mind. The father, a term used only in a biological sense, also had to give consent. But the pregnancy was irresponsible in the first place, and now the boy was being asked to be responsible.

The doctor was not helpful. He wanted to "save money" by delivering the baby in his home. Contrary to common advice, the girl wanted to have her baby naturally, hold him, name him, and feed him. It was her choice.

It is easy to understand why agency adoptions are preferred by the systems over private adoptions.

Through their lawyer the couple sent the hospital payments a week prior to the due date. The girl agreed it would be best to leave her baby in the hospital. She refused to permit foster parents to care for her child, even for a few hours. The parents were to pick up the baby at the hospital. The hospital administration and staff agreed, finally.

I am sure many babies are born on their due dates or before. This precious little girl was born a week and a half late. Thank the Lord she was fine and the mother was fine. Again, despite advice, the mother held, named, and fed her baby. She had seventy-two hours before she could sign the legal consent form.

She held her daughter so close. The baby never cried at all; the mother never stopped crying. She repeated over and over, "I love you enough to give you away. You will have a better life than Mommy." It was so quiet, so very quiet in her room.

The nurses were terrific. The maids cleaned a room specifically for the meeting. Father Selle and I arrived at ten minutes to nine to make sure all was well. The mother's family had not arrived. The nurses combed the baby's fine little hairs and taped on a tiny bow. The baby looked even smaller and more precious, if that were possible.

The mother didn't want to wait any longer for her parents. Fifteen minutes was long enough. After all, they had "never done anything for her," why would they show love for her baby? Father Selle read some prayers.

I read from 1 Samuel 2, for this was a child we had all prayed over for months, and now she was being given.

Father Selle anointed the tiny head as the baby was held so tightly and lovingly by the mother. The nurses supported her as much as they could. The prayer of dedication was one of praise, thanksgiving, and a request for a special outpouring of grace.

Mother and baby spent three minutes, eighteen seconds alone. The door opened and she said again, "I love you, Baby. I love you so much I am doing this." She kissed the baby, bathing her with tears. Then she handed me the baby, clothed in the blanket she had made. The baby was given to the nurse.

I wheeled the mother out of the hospital. Hospital elevators have to be the world's slowest. The mother went to stay with some of our friends.

Of course, it was raining the next morning when we met at probate court. The referee spent an appropriate amount of time and longer. The girl was emotional but definite. Her lawyer was polite, efficient, hurried, and unfeeling.

The papers were ready by noon. It was 12:30 when I walked back into the hospital. The new mother and father were easily visible in the lobby. The weather was rather cool—but the precious little one really did not require three beautiful handmade quilts. As I sat down, I asked the couple how they were—an empty time-filler question. I commented upon the weather, as three nurses commented upon the quilts. Bob told me that they would give me thirty more seconds before great bodily harm would occur.

I gave Bob a key chain, Jane a locket, each holding a picture of their baby. Then the head nurse arrived to escort us up to the baby. She looked as though she had somehow grown in one day. As the head nurse was explaining to Jane about feeding, another nurse slowly walked up carrying the baby. And, oh, that moment! Mother met baby; baby met mother. Finally, Jane proclaimed, "She's beautiful!"

145

Because of Jane's trembling hands, the nurse dressed the baby. By divine providence, I'm sure, a friend who is an obstetrician released the baby, which eliminated a hassle. Only smiles were present as a nurse carried the bright-eyed baby out of the hospital to begin a happy future surrounded by total love. Even our prayer of thanksgiving seemed understated.

Giving up a baby for adoption requires an abundance of love, maturity, strength, and the epitome of selflessness.

Certainly God designed his creation according to a definite plan, and told us what is best. He commanded against adultery and fornication. It is the effects of the sin that I see daily in dealing with youth and adults. Sex with many partners lowers self-esteem; no love is involved. One of the reasons for so much divorce is too-early sexual experience. Sex is meant to be an adult act. Youth who engage in it thoughtlessly lose the fun of adolescence too quickly.

We need to be realistic about couples who have been having frequent and pleasurable sexual experiences. Simply to say "stop" is unrealistic. This is where personal standards are really needed for self-control and responsible behavior. When a boy challenges, "If you love me you will prove it," a girl may well respond, "If you really loved me, you wouldn't even ask."

A child should be openly praised for doing other things rather than engaging in sex. It is appropriate for a couple to thank each other for not having sex. Youth in love must openly and honestly face their sexual desires and then realistically and creatively develop alternative Christian behavior. The activities, of course, vary with the couples. A strong church youth activities program is essential. It provides a way of escape.

No temptation has seized youth which is not common to human experience, but God is faithful and will not let them be tempted beyond what they can bear. He will offer a way of escape so that they will be able to bear it. (See 1 Corinthians 10:12, 13.)

God's redemptive action in Jesus Christ makes ethical sexual behavior possible. Paul encourages, "I can do all things through Christ which strengtheneth me" (Philippians 4:13, KJV). " . . . He has granted to us his precious and very great promises, that through these you may escape from the corruption that is in the world because of passion and become partakers of the divine nature. For this very reason you make every effort to supplement your faith with virtue, and virtue with knowledge, and knowledge with self-control, and self-control with steadfastness, and steadfastness with godliness, and godliness with brotherly affection, and brotherly affection with love" (2 Peter 1:4-7, RSV).

Scripture warns us against sexual immorality. "For this is the will of God, your sanctification: that you abstain from unchastity; that each one of you know how to take a wife for himself in holiness and honor, not in the passion of lust like heathen who do not know God; that no man transgress, and wrong his brother in this matter, because the Lord is an avenger in all these things, as we solemnly forewarned you. For God has not called us for uncleanness, but in holiness. Therefore, whoever disregards this disregards not man but God, who gives his Holy Spirit to you" (1 Thessalonians 4:3-8, RSV).

Of course, God is willing to forgive sin, including sexual sin.

As parents we frankly teach our child the beauty of the sexual relationship as clearly as his age permits him to understand. We instill the biblical truths. We help pattern in him responsible sexual behavior, just as we help pattern all responsible behavior. We motivate the child to avoid situations of temptation and to become involved in positive, meaningful alternative behavior that God will bless.

THE DRUG-ABUSING CHILD

> As the father has loved me, so have I loved you; abide in my love. If you keep my commandments, you will abide in my love, just as I have kept my Father's commandments and abide in his love. (John 15:9, 10, RSV)

Scared straight. Often chemical abuse is a symptom of feeling the lack of love, faith, fun, and hope. For some, drugs become fun, at least for a while. Basically, with this role-oriented generation, kids can be "scared straight" for a little while—but not for long, and some who are good kids already can be scared to be better. But the love of Christ and of the family lasts when fear fades. The child who takes drugs needs to pray.

Jason thought we had been to "too many" places looking for a job for him. He gave big hints about how he wanted to "have it his way," so we ended up at Burger King. As we ordered our Whoppers, I noticed that the young man behind the counter stared and then almost smiled at me.

One of the sandwiches he gave us was huge. When we sat down, Jason grabbed his Whopper and asked what in the world I had ordered. It had four beef patties, four slices of tomato, lettuce all over, and mayonnaise gushing out. As I tried to figure out whether to stuff all that in my mouth or go back to the counter to ask what it was, I noticed that the young man was standing at our table.

"Do you like your Whopper-whopper-whopper?" he asked.

"It's huge."

"Well," he said and then sang, "Aren't you hungry?"

He asked if he could join us. Sure. His name tag indicated he was the manager; it was his place, so we would be glad for him to join us.

I did not recognize him. He said his name was Ryan. He asked Jason if I was still telling those dumb stories.

Jason too impulsively laughed.

"Ryan, I believe we have met before," I said.

"Oh, yes, before and before, and before that, too," he offered with bowed head.

The last time had been five years ago when he was in detention. Ryan related how I had told a "dumb story" in chapel about a boy who drank too much. Ryan said I challenged the detained teens that, if they took drugs, they should ask God to help them.

Ryan said he had thought the statement was the world's dumbest. He didn't need help.

Ryan continued his story; the day he left the court at age fifteen, he ran away. He made it to somewhere in Indiana, where he immediately started to "party" with alcohol and drugs.

Ryan was having difficulty continuing the story. I tried to eat some of the lettuce.

He said he did not know what had happened or for how long he had blacked out. He woke up in a closet with intense pain. He felt his face and knew his jaw was broken. He had excruciating pain in his left arm. Through the little light that was creeping in through the ajar door, he saw dried blood on his clothes. But then, to his terror, he realized they weren't his clothes. He was panic-stricken.

Ryan looked up; his red eyes met mine. He continued that in the panic he remembered my "drunk" story and he prayed for help. As he prayed he heard footsteps. His heart pounded faster. He couldn't move. The pain, oh, the pain.

The door slowly opened. An older gentleman bent over him and asked if he was all right.

Ryan stayed in the hospital for two months. When he got out, he developed alternative behavior. He lived with the gentleman, got a job, went back to school, became active in a good church. After three years he returned to Akron, a new man.

He said, "And look, I have made something of myself; I'm the manager. I can make Whopper-whopper-whoppers."

He reached over, gripped my arm, and pleaded, "Please, Byron, challenge kids that if they take drugs they need to pray." Softly, he testified, "Your stories are good. Please keep telling them." I am.

Whenever groups sing for our chapel services, the members comment that the detained youth look so normal—just like any other kids. Of course, in a sense, they are. Yet many people wonder why young, energetic, good-looking kids hurt themselves by taking drugs.

When I sustained a neck injury in an auto accident, I experienced a great deal of pain. The doctor in the emergency room of the hospital pulled on my head. It really hurt. He told me there was something wrong with my neck. Smart doctor.

I could have done many things. I could have been delinquent and pulled on his neck. I could have gotten depressed and prayed, "Why me?" I could have become philosophical and asked God why there is evil in the world and why people get sick, why people die, and why are there car wrecks. All this would not have helped the pain in my neck.

I could have said,"Go ahead, pull on my neck. It's not mine, it's George's." Then he would have sought to admit me to the psychiatric unit. I could have become hostile and smashed all the oxygen equipment. I could have chosen from many different alternative behaviors.

The doctor told me that after I took a medication I would not feel the pain anymore. The pain was intense, so without hesitation, I took the medication. Sometimes when the pain within our children becomes too great, they do not hesitate—they take drugs.

THE ALCOHOLIC CHILD

For you shall go out in joy, and be led forth in peace. (Isaiah 55:12, RSV)

Drunk nine-year-old. Probably the greatest increase in alcohol consumption is occurring among elementary students. I am disturbed at the increasing numbers of younger youth being referred for intoxication.

It was about 11:00 P.M. when the policeman carried a nine-year-old boy into the court. He was too drunk to walk. He had passed out after being put in a holding room. I sat with him and waited.

After ten minutes he opened his eyes and looked around. He saw me and saw the cross around my neck. He was startled and began to cry. He whispered, "Oh, my God, I died."

I smiled and softly reassured,"No, you are only in juvenile court."

He responded, "I wish I had died."

As we talked into the night, he recounted how he began drinking when he was "little," after school before his parents got home. He was sure they knew, but they never said anything. The parents, according to him, did not care.

151

The little kid realized how manipulative he had become, but he rationalized he had to be that way to get his "stuff." Once the father had said something vague about it being better to drink than to smoke pot, and thus the boy felt the father's approval. Of course, the father was wrong, very wrong. It took a long family conference, and work alone with this boy, to get him the help he needed to fight this too-soon-learned addiction.

Many school systems, mental health organizations, churches, and parent groups have spent thousands of hours and dollars to fight the battle of the drug-abusing child. Much of what has been done has been effective. Referrals related to drugs are decreasing. Many groups consider this victory and take much credit. But closer examination of the statistics is necessary.

Referrals for alcohol abuse are increasing. Referrals for auto theft and grand theft have increased. Violent crime has increased, particularly among girls. Students report on the average that roughly 75 percent of their peers drink at least two beers a week. This is alarming. And 20 percent are considered by peers to have a serious drinking problem. A third of the high school students get drunk at least once a week. Mr. Neal Verity, Chief Referee, Summit County Juvenile Court, has often called alcohol the number one problem. Probably over 80 percent of all adolescents arrested on criminal charges drink before committing crimes. Almost half of all assaults by juveniles are committed under the influence of alcohol.

Kids do not just drop out of school anymore. Many drop into alcohol abuse. They can't find jobs; they don't have anything to do. What little money they can somehow get together, they spend on the "fun in the bottle."

And whatever you ask in prayer, you will receive, if you have faith. (Matthew 21:22, RSV)

After-school drinker. It is possible for kids to stop drinking.

Jerry's visits over an eight-month period had been "spontaneous," as he called them. He dropped into the court at about lunchtime, as usual. As I watched him "pig out" on a bucket of chicken, he asked me if I thought he drank too much. He was reluctant to relate how much he drank until after I had paid the lunch bill. He said he drank "three or four" each afternoon as soon as he got home from school. He drank a few more during the evening and began his day with "one or two."

I could have told him about hundreds of other kids who were washed away. I asked him what he thought.

"Too much."

I emphatically agreed. Jerry stopped cleaning the chicken bones and started playing with them. I waited. He asked with great intensity, "How can I quit?"

I asked if he knew anyone who didn't drink. It took him several minutes to think of a fellow student who didn't drink, but who was also very religious and a "nerd." I think it would have been easier to get the secret recipe for the chicken's herbs and spices than to get the kid to see he needed the "nerd."

Jerry dropped by just before lunch a week later. He was really happy. He had met the new friend for four afternoons after school. He said, "Right then and there the three of us prayed that we wouldn't drink, and we haven't and we won't." Huge smile.

I was excited. I asked him who the third person was.

Jerry looked me straight in the eye and said, "God, dummy."

As parents we help our kids to learn how to have fun. We guide them in selecting friends. But the final responsibility of "to drink or not to drink" rests with the kid.

We need to be careful not to overreact to an already bad situation, and thereby make it worse. When we suspect chemical abuse, we should examine the characteristics of love, faith, fun, and hope. We look for a change in attitude, grades, friends, eating and sleeping habits, interests, and motivation. Calmly, carefully, prayerfully, lovingly, tactfully, we help fill in the gaps.

ALTERNATIVE BEHAVIOR

> If you confess with your lips that Jesus is Lord and believe in your heart that God raised him from the dead, you will be saved. (Romans 10:9, 10, RSV)

Sometimes it is as if we as a society must make a choice. Either our kids are going to be pacified by drugs or they are going to be violent by drink. As referrals for drugs increase, violent crime decreases. As violent crime referrals decrease, drug referrals increase. But by God's grace, there is an alternative. We should never take anything away from a child without helping him to put something better in its place. We cannot just naively say, "Don't drink, don't smoke pot, don't have sex, don't be delinquent, don't be unruly." We must help the child find alternative behaviors that are positive and fulfilling.

Alternative behavior must include the power of Jesus Christ and the power of the family. Salvation is the experience whereby the guilt and sins are taken away, but the person is not left empty; he is filled with the presence of the Holy Spirit. We must help our children to replace drugs,

154

alcohol, and other vices with the fulfillment of a genuine religious experience.

Belief in the Lord Jesus Christ is an alternative behavior. The child who is saved replaces a bad life style with a good one. Jesus Christ brings the peace and fulfillment youth want and need.

Detention boy's salvation. As I walked in, I noticed the frown on his face. Kevin looked the other way as I approached. Then he jerked his head around, quickly walked up to me, and shouted, "Are you a preacher?"

My affirmation only increased his anger.

He grabbed my cross and proclaimed, boldly, "I don't believe in God."

I introduced myself and called him by name. He was surprised I knew his name. I explained that his court hearing had been changed, and that I had come to escort him to the courtroom.

His anger changed to fear, and he immediately pleaded, "Oh, preacher, please pray for me."

I told him I would be glad to, but I wanted to pray with him.

"That would be fine," he said, with almost a smile.

I could not resist chiding, "Well, now, you said that you don't believe in God. Whom shall we pray to?"

He whispered, "Oh, you know I just have to say things like that in here."

"I know," I said, as I put my hand on his shoulder. Was he ever trembling!

"OK," he asked impatiently, "how do we pray?"

First I thanked God for the boy; then for his holy presence and strength. I instructed the boy to pray as he felt led.

He bowed his head and prayed, "God, wow, this is awful!"

Good, honest prayer. He raised his eyes to mine, then above to the ceiling, and with an excited tone he uttered, mostly to himself, "I almost believed that if I ever prayed, the ceiling would fall in."

"There's more," I offered.

"What?"

"You have hurt some people; your parents, yourself, and God."

Again he quickly agreed, so he asked for forgiveness for breaking into the home, the crime on his police report.

I raised my head. He said, ashamed, "There's more."

He prayed for forgiveness about a home we did not know he had broken into. We learn a lot through prayer. As he finished, he smiled, asking, "Is there more?"

"The toughest part," I said. "What about the future?"

"Oh, yeah," he said. "God, help me never to break into any more houses forever."

I added, "And this week is a part of forever, especially this week."

The boy was placed on probation and was released from detention. He said he would call me the next day. He didn't.

I was disappointed. I had hoped so much that he was sincere.

A week later he called in the middle of the night. He was out of breath and really angry. He had tried to break into a house. He had put the tape on the window and was ready to smash it in. Then he said, "I couldn't believe it; I just could not believe it! I thought I saw your face in the window. I was scared to death. Then I remembered our prayer."

He continued, "Please don't tell any of my friends, but I took the tape off the window and I ran home to call you." He thought I had put a curse on him. We talked, and prayed—this time sincerely.

Over half of the youth referred to the court for intoxication have not eaten a meal with their families during the previous six months. Maybe they didn't want to; maybe they didn't feel welcome. Maybe the parents were equally frustrated thinking the youth did not want to do anything with them.

Parents should strive to plan for recreational activities with their children. All kids like to shop, as well. One of the goals I present most frequently to parents during the first session is to ask them to sit near their child as the child watches TV. I ask them to smile at the child during the commercials. That way at least the parents will get some of the child's attention. As they smile during the first commercial, the child will move farther down the couch, in the opposite direction. As the parents smile during the second commercial, the child might mumble something under his breath to the effect, "I knew it would happen someday." During the third commercial, the child will not be able to take it any longer and will blurt out, "What do you want?"

The prayers are answered; the opportunity for direct communication has arrived.

The parents say, "After this show, let's plan some things we can do together." Maybe all you can plan is simply to eat a meal together. But a relationship activity is planned. The family might also plan a recreational activity or a family visit. This seems so simplistic when measured against heavy tension and complex situations. But when the kid finally smiles while he eats, the process toward healing has begun.

Baby steps. When our baby, Trina, first started to cry, Ann or I would pick her up, comfort her, and heal all problems. She sensed the love and security and stopped crying. We handled a problem if there was one. It is true, too, that a

157

kiss "makes it better." We gave her a favorite toy. At least the activity diverted her attention.

When Trina started to touch the oven, we shouted, "No!" We also handed her some pots and pans. As our children grow, we still need to help divert their attention into more positive alternative behavior.

Trina stood one day, tottering back and forth. I sat, arms outstretched, only a few inches from her, proclaiming with all confidence, "Come to Daddy; you can do it." She walked a step. I picked her up and squeezed her with love. I moved back a few inches. After much serious deliberation and dialogue, she took two steps. Again the squeals and squeezes. I moved back four feet. She watched me carefully, and then sank to the floor and buried her head in her hands. Too far, too much, too fast. The alternative behavior must be reachable or total frustration will set in. Later that same evening Laura, age ten, discussed tryouts for a school musical. She needed the "Come on, you can do it," even more than the baby. I wonder if, when she first backs the car out of the garage, I am going to be at the end of the driveway, saying, "Come on, you can make it."

This is the encouragement our children need—all of their lives.

CONCLUSION

Whoever drinks of the water that I shall give him will never thirst; the water that I shall give him will become in him a spring of water welling up to eternal life. (John 4:14, RSV)

Many times Jesus clearly presented the way toward a better life. From the fourth chapter of the Gospel of John, we learn how Jesus had occasion to talk with a woman about God's love. He presented a better life to a woman in Samaria. Jesus knew she had something to give—a drink of water. Jesus felt the woman had worth, although this woman was likely depressed—as she revealed by coming to the well around high noon. She probably did not want to talk to anyone or be reminded of her past.

Jesus did not talk about her past; he talked about the present. The woman wanted Jesus to leave. At first she insulted him, pretended to be ignorant; still, Jesus continued his involvement with her. Jesus used the present tense when he indicated in verse 10, "If you knew the gift of God, and who it is that is saying to you, 'Give me a drink,' you would have asked him, and he would have given you living water" (RSV).

As the woman continued to talk with him, Jesus said to her, "Go, call your husband." Jesus was pointing out the present situation. The woman answered, "I have no husband."

Jesus did not judge her, condemn her, or ridicule her. He praised her: "You are right." The woman felt there was something very different about this Man; so, perhaps, she felt that he did have something to offer her.

She wanted a plan. She asked about worship and Jesus told her plainly of the need to worship the Father in spirit and in truth.

The woman wanted to commit herself to him and said that she would learn from him all things. When she spoke of the Messiah, Jesus told her, "I who speak to you am he." One of the first proclamations Jesus made that he was the Son of God was to this woman at the well, because he cared about her as an individual.

He presented a plan which she accepted. Her commitment was seen in the fact that she left the fountain and ran to the village to tell everyone about Jesus.

The woman had begun by coming to the well at noon so that she would not have to see anyone; she left running into the village to tell everyone of her new life. Her behavior changed because of the power of God working in her life. Of extreme importance is the fact that Jesus never gave up; three times the woman tried to get him to go away; but he remained. Her commitment came in response to his concern and love.

Free fries for life. A sixteen-year-old boy whom I met in detention very much needed Christ's living water. Jeff had been in detention so often that his name had become a "detentionhold" word. At the age of fourteen he had been in fourteen foster homes and now he was being released to yet another one. He was anxious and extremely depressed, suicidal.

I took him to lunch. Wendy's restaurant was running a contest. The boy got a card picturing three French fries in a row. Jeff won some free fries! He was so excited. He had never won anything before. God knew he needed to be a winner.

Since I was paying for lunch, he kept the card. He left with his foster parents that afternoon. It was rather late the next evening when the phone rang. Silence.

I was ready to hang up when I heard a weak voice say, "You want some fries?" I immediately knew it was Jeff and asked where he was. I really rushed to the Wendy's to find he had only one French fry left to eat. He told me I should have hurried. It was tough for him to make that last fry last. He kept dipping it in ketchup and then licking it off.

He told me he had lots of napkins, and besides, he didn't think the triple burgers were too hot and juicy for him. I considered his statement to be a hint to me. Jeff went on to say that he didn't think it was too cold for a frostie, either.

We got triples and frosties. As we sat down, he asked if I would say the blessing. As I simply asked God to bless the boy and the food, I heard him begin to cry. He was using up all his napkins. I waited and watched his frostie get warm and his triple get cold.

Finally, he regained enough composure to reach into his jacket pocket. He pulled out a folded, torn, dirty index card. Jeff unfolded it and revealed a rusty razor blade. He said he had been on his way to the park to kill himself when he reached into his pocket for the folded card. But instead he found the Wendy's card. He had thought maybe I would share his last meal—an order of fries.

As I asked the blessing, Jeff realized God was there. We had triples, frosties, and fries every lunch for eight days. On the eighth day he asked if he could pray with me.

As an old minister friend of mine said, "We keep on keeping on." The fervent prayer of the righteous does prevail.